Ocean Cruising Survey

Ocean Cruising Survey

An Appraisal of Boats, Gear and Crew

JIMMY CORNELL

SHERIDAN HOUSE

Published in the United States of America 1986 by
Sheridan House Inc., 145 Palisade St, Dobbs Ferry,
New York 10522

First published in Great Britain by
Granada Publishing in Adlard Coles Ltd 1983
under the title *Modern Ocean Cruising*
Second edition published by
Adlard Coles Ltd, 8 Grafton Street, London W1X 3LA

Library of Congress Cataloging in Publication Data
Cornell, Jimmy
Ocean Cruising survey: an appraisal of boats,
gear and crew.—2nd ed.
1. Yachts and yachting
I. Title   II. Cornell, Jimmy. Modern ocean
cruising,
791.1′24   GV813

ISBN 0–911378–56–1

Printed and bound in Great Britain

FOR GWENDA

Many ocean cruises owe their success
to the seawife as much as to the skipper.
This book is dedicated to my seawife,
without whom it would never have
been written.

Contents

3   *Living Afloat – the Practical and Administrative Aspects*   60

4   *Aspects of Seamanship*   85

List of Maps and Diagrams

Foreword

Sitting at a desk at the centre of a busy yachting magazine office may not give many opportunities to go ocean cruising, but it does give an unrivalled opportunity to read about other peoples' exploits. Articles, letters, telephone calls even, on occasion, the people themselves come into the office.

A great deal of personal experience and personal preference is included in all those individual items and it has always seemed to me to be a great pity that *Yachting World* could only publish a very small amount of the material available and certainly we found it impossible to collate the vast store of information that was there. When Jimmy Cornell came into my office, however, all that changed.

Here was one person who had not only ocean cruising experience, but also a reporter's training and inquisitiveness. Not for him the simple feat of a six year circumnavigation with a young family, but while he was out there exploring the world he was also exploring the store of information carried by his fellow cruising people.

Jimmy has managed to collect the flavour of all those articles that came into the *Yachting World* office, the anecdotes, the narrative items, but has also managed to intersperse a vast storehouse of detail and facts. You know that the information on anchors or echo sounders that comes from the experience of hundreds of people who have travelled tens of thousands of miles in small sailing boats just has to be believed.

Sitting down with Jimmy and talking about the results of his surveys always leads us on to the design of his next boat, planned for a forthcoming return to the Pacific. Plans and ideas are examined, and he is forever visiting one boatyard after another to see if *this* will be the boat.

Jimmy has taken the findings of his surveys to heart. Next time his boat will either be aluminium or steel, cutter rigged rather than ketch and I am sure the equipment and layout will reflect many of the lessons that have come up through his surveys.

Future long distance sailors who have the benefit of this book will be better prepared and better equipped for what they will meet.

Dick Johnson
Editor, *Yachting World*

Introduction

Ocean voyaging is no longer the privilege of the few or the extraordinary, as more and more people undertake extended cruises across the oceans of the world. Over the years the design of boats has changed considerably, new materials have become available, instruments have reached a high level of sophistication and even old established concepts of seamanship have come under scrutiny. However the sea and the challenge it presents to the ocean voyager has remained the same. This challenge is one reason why many people put to sea. Cruising to faraway places has other attractions too, besides a desire to battle with the elements; it is also a means of escaping from the frustrations and stresses of modern society. Fortunately there are still many places which can only be reached by sea and the satisfaction of sailing one's own boat to such a place makes every sacrifice worthwhile. Many ocean voyagers are pursuing a dream and few of those who manage to realise it are disillusioned. To make this dream come true requires a lot of preparation and determination, and the ultimate success of a long distance cruise often depends on these initial preparations.

In pursuit of the dream of freedom myself, I started serious preparation for a world cruise in the early 1970s. I chose a Trintella III A, designed by Van de Stadt, for its sturdiness and suitable accommodation for a family with two young children. A limited budget forced me to buy just the bare hull, but fortunately I insisted on the best I could afford and the strong fibreglass hull built by the Tyler Boat Company has proved its worth on many occasions. After two years of fitting out the 36-footer, we set off from England in the spring of 1975. Six years later *Aventura* successfully completed her circumnavigation, having taken myself, my wife Gwenda and children Doina and Ivan on a voyage of 58,000 miles during which we visited over 50 countries in five continents.

When I left London I gave up my job with the BBC External Service, although I continued my radio work on a freelance basis throughout the voyage. This work encouraged me to visit many out of the way places; what started off as a three year trip took twice as long to complete. Like countless sailors before us, the South Seas cast their spell and if it hadn't been for the problem of our growing children's education, *Aventura* would still be sailing among the islands of the South Pacific.

When I started preparing for my voyage, I had little cruising experience, so I read avidly every available book on this subject. There were several books on the market, but most of them had one major drawback, they reflected the point of view of only one person, the author. They tended to be subjective, sometimes dogmatic, and seldom gave alternative points of view a good hearing.

After several years of sailing in the company of people who have made cruising their way of life, I came to realise that there was a fund of knowledge from these experienced sailors waiting to be tapped. Not wanting to fall into the same trap of preaching from the cockpit, I decided to try and let these sailors tell me their own stories.

My training as a radio reporter showed me the obvious way, which was to let the people talk and for me to listen. The result of some three years of listening to countless skippers, mates and crews is included in these pages. In an attempt to be objective I carried out several surveys on specific subjects among the long distance cruising people that I encountered during my own voyage around the world. Each survey was based on a detailed questionnaire and the interviews were conducted in a systematic fashion. Wherever possible I tried to interview people on their own, preferably on their boats, as I found that people spoke more freely and honestly when others were not around. I attempted to process some of the data from the questionnaires in a simple statistical way by averaging figures and calculating percentages.

Although I tried to make the questionnaires as comprehensive and wide ranging as possible, some aspects had to be left out and when some of those interviewed felt strongly about certain overlooked points, I made a note of these. At the end of each interview, I also asked for general comments relating to the subjects under discussion and suggestions for others intending long distance voyages. Some of the most valuable information came to light in this way.

These 'surveys', as I call them, carried out over a number of years, form the basis of this book. Generally I have endeavoured to present the data resulting from the surveys in an unbiased way, only interpreting it when necessary. Of course I hold strong opinions myself on most of these matters, so I have tried to make it clear when I stray across the thin line of objectivity by expressing my own views or making a certain point by drawing on my own experience.

But nothing stands still in this world, least of all in ocean cruising, where new ideas and equipment are introduced all the time. In order to update the information contained in this book I returned to the South Pacific to interview a new sample of long distance voyagers on the latest trends in cruising

MAP A Track of *Aventura*'s voyage

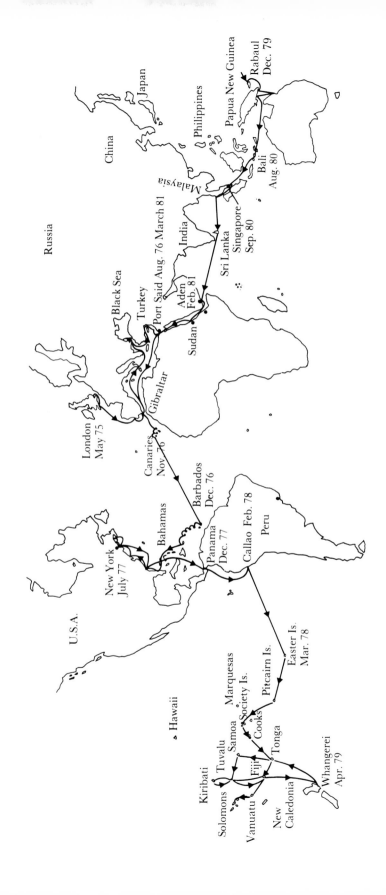

matters. A vast amount of new material was gathered, some of which reinforced the lessons learned from earlier interviews, while some shed new light on certain aspects of ocean voyaging. I was thus able to drastically revise the first edition of this book and bring it completely up to date.

Over the last six years I have interviewed more than two hundred skippers and their mates on all aspects of cruising, the information being contained in five main surveys:

1. *The Suva Survey.* The first survey of 62 cruising boats was conducted entirely in Suva, Fiji and dealt with various aspects of cruising boat design.

2. *The Cruising Survey.* The following year in a variety of places in the Pacific I conducted a more extensive survey among fifty long distance cruising boats. This dealt particularly with aspects of seamanship and the practical side of cruising.

3. *The Seawives Survey.* A separate survey was conducted parallel to the Cruising Survey among the cruising women.

4. *The Circumnavigation.* Twelve crews who had successfully completed their circumnavigation rounded off this series of surveys.

5. *The Pacific Survey.* Fifty skippers were interviewed in the South Pacific at the end of 1984 on a comprehensive range of subjects with a particular focus on gear and instrumentation.

Tables showing the details of all these surveys are at the end of the book.

Although I gathered most of my material in the Pacific, I consider it applicable to any cruising area of the world. The people sailing in the Pacific are nearly all long distance voyagers, both they and their boats are well tried, their crews being committed to living aboard for long periods of time. They are all used to long offshore passages as distances in the Pacific are so vast that a 1000 mile passage between islands is commonplace. At the same time those cruising in the South Pacific have few facilities at their disposal, such as rescue services, port and repair facilities, navigational aids, even detailed and accurate charts. Of necessity in the Pacific, the sailor has to be more self-reliant.

Many of the people I interviewed had also sailed extensively in other oceans and the information they gave me was based on knowledge gained worldwide. Apart from these surveys, I have also drawn extensively from general conversations I have had with many skippers and letters written by the people concerned. There are many interesting people sailing the oceans of the world and they all have a story to tell. This is their tale.

CHAPTER ONE

In Search of the Ideal Boat

There are certain ports on the crossroads of the oceans rarely missed by any long distance cruising boats and one of these is Suva, the capital of Fiji. In September and October this excellent port, conveniently placed halfway across the South Pacific, is particularly crowded as the safe cruising season draws to its close and the cyclone season approaches. Many boats are preparing for a passage to New Zealand or Australia out of the cyclone area, while others staying in Suva find themselves a protected corner close to a hurricane hole to sit out the season.

Looking at the variety of boats anchored off the hospitable Royal Suva Yacht Club set me wondering where all the ideal blue water cruising boats

The anchorage off the Royal Suva Yacht Club, Fiji, a meeting place for long distance cruising boats.

were, those advertised in the glossy magazines and exhibited at boat shows. Maybe they were all cosily tucked away in expensive marinas in Europe and North America, certainly those sailing the oceans were a motley collection of different shapes, sizes and rigs, old and new, big and small.

In a search for the 'ideal' long distance cruising boat, I decided to try and find out in a statistical way what boats people were actually cruising in, and more importantly, what they thought about their boats. Hopefully, with a large enough sample general conclusions could be drawn. Suva was an ideal place to begin and I tried to interview the skipper of every long distance cruising boat that came through during my own three month stay there.

Choosing the Sample

Only boats which had sailed a minimum of 2000 miles or who had been cruising for over three months were interviewed and sixty-two boats made up my first survey. In fact I soon discovered that most of the boats had been sailing for much further and longer, most of them over one year and up to fifteen years continuous cruising in the case of *Coryphena*. Three of the boats, *Warna Carina*, *Ben Gunn*, and *Sarrie*, were completing their circumnavigation, while Seaton Grass was taking his father's ketch *Merry Maiden* around the world a second time, having learned the ropes on a previous circumnavigation skippered by his father. The mileage covered by the boats on their present cruise worked out at an average of 15,000 miles per boat and the average length of the cruise so far was 2·6 years. It was soon apparent that many skippers were even more experienced, having sailed extensively before the present cruise. The sailing experience of all the skippers added up to a total of 856 years, quite a biblical age, being an average of 13·8 years per skipper. This considerable experience, together with the length of the cruises currently being undertaken gives immense authority to the answers obtained.

Size of Boat

The first thing I looked at was the size of the boats, which varied between two schooners over 70 ft long to a small sloop of only 24 ft. When I asked the skippers to give a rating to the design and sailing performance of their boats, I asked them to also take into account the size of the boat for the number of crew carried. Children were only counted as crew when they lived permanently on board and crews joining a boat for a limited period were excluded. The ratings were counted from one to ten, ten being the highest rating.

TABLE 1. *Results of optimum size questionnaire, Suva Survey.*

Length (ft)	Number of boats	Average number of crew	Average rating
under 35 ft	12	2	7·75
35–40 ft	22	2·5	9·27
40–45 ft	12	2·4	8·83
over 45 ft	16	3·5	9·25

The happiest skippers were those of boats in the 35–40 ft range (see Table 1) who rated their boats at an average of 9·27. The skippers of the twelve smaller boats, under 35 ft, gave their boats a lower rating of 7·75. Although the boats over 45 ft also received a high average rating, many of these had larger crews and in several cases where the crew consisted only of a couple, these skippers complained that their boats were too large to handle. For this reason, some of the larger boats took on temporary crew for longer passages.

The following year, during my second survey, consisting of fifty boats, the average cruising boat turned out to be in the same range, 38 ft long and with an average crew of 2·4.

Later, in a survey of twelve boats which had successfully completed their circumnavigation, mostly with a crew of two people, I found the boats to be of a slightly smaller size, on average 35 ft. Of these twelve, only two were over 40 ft, while three were under 30 ft. Asked to give an overall assessment of their boats, every single skipper specified that he was happy with his boat, having made the right choice for the voyage he undertook and the money he had available. That these twelve circumnavigating skippers were satisfied with their particular boat was to be expected, for these were the successes, not the failures, and their boats had all brought them safely back home. However out of these twelve, only four planned to keep their present boat, whilst all the other eight were planning or already building slightly larger boats for the future. Jean-Francois Delvaux of *Alkinoos*, who has sailed his 48 ft ketch virtually single-handed around the world, considers a boat of 38–40 ft long to be ideal for a world cruise. His view is shared by Herbert Gieseking, who has sailed many thousands of miles on his various boats named *Lou*. After the completion of a successful circumnavigation on 31 ft *Lou IV*, he built *Lou V*, a 40 ft steel ketch, on which he and his wife Illa have left for an open ended voyage.

It has often been said that a short-handed crew should try and keep to a small boat, possibly under 35 ft overall. The Suva survey however showed that with only three exceptions every owner of a boat under 35 ft long complained

Jimmy Cornell interviewing Liisa and Einar Einarsson on *Irma* in Whangarei. Whenever possible the interviews took place on the boat in question.

about the small size and stated unreservedly that he would have preferred to have had a larger boat for this type of cruising. As to the difficulty of handling a larger boat, it was interesting to note that not a single boat in the 35–46 ft range with a crew of two was considered too difficult to handle, even in the worst conditions. Perhaps I should add that a lot of the crews were not all that young either, several being in their sixties. Alan Allmark, who has been cruising many years on his 35 ft *Telemark*, advised those choosing a long distance cruising boat, 'Don't go for a bigger boat than you might need and most certainly do not buy a large boat just because you can afford it.'

Obviously the choice of the size of a boat depends greatly on the number of people who will be cruising in her. Bill and Frances Stocks were quite happy with their 30 ft cutter *Kleena Kleene II* until the birth of their daughter in Papua New Guinea, an event not foreseen when they had left British Columbia a few years previously. The boat then appeared to shrink rapidly as the pile of baby paraphernalia grew. Similarly *Warna Carina* left Australia with three small children aboard, but completed the circumnavigation with three large teenagers. By the time they had reached Suva, this family of five were finding their 36 ft boat overcrowded. Growing children do take up more space, and this is a factor to be considered in the choice of a family boat.

Alan and Beryl Allmark have been cruising for many years on their 35 ft *Telemark*. They consider this to be an ideal size for a small crew.

Long distance cruising boats usually spend more time at anchor than at sea, and this is when more space is important. Even in the tropics, where one may expect to spend most of the time in the open, an airy interior and spacious galley are essential. From the number of cruising folk who sleep in the cockpit on hot tropical nights, a large and comfortable cockpit would appear to be popular, also pleasant for entertaining visitors from other boats and from ashore. A cruising boat, after all, is a home as well as a sailing machine.

The often debated point of a centre versus an after cockpit seemed to be dictated often by size of the boat, more of the smaller boats having an after cockpit than the larger ones. The people who had a centre cockpit and an after cabin all appeared pleased with this arrangement, often for the privacy gained when they had a crew. My own boat has a centre cockpit, which I always regarded as safer and more secure when my children were young, a point which has been mentioned to me by several parents. Otherwise the positioning of the cockpit did not appear to be a major consideration among those surveyed.

What was more important was that the helmsman had some sort of protection. In the Suva survey, six boats had a permanent doghouse or wheelhouse, while forty were provided with some kind of canvas dodger, which also gave protection to the main companionway and was usually left in position, even if it could be folded away. All skippers agreed that a protected steering position was an essential fixture on any cruising boat however much one relied on selfsteering or autopilot. Almost all of the few skippers who had unprotected cockpits wished that they had some protection and mentioned that it was high on their list of jobs to be done at the first opportunity. Practically all the boats had a tent or awning of some kind, to be used mostly while not sailing as a protection against sun and rain.

A shortcoming often found in the design of boats is insufficient ventilation. This is not only a problem related to the tropics, as several skippers complained of the lack of ventilation on their boats while sailing in poor weather conditions when they had to keep the hatches closed. In the Pacific survey, fifteen skippers considered that they did not have sufficient hatches or ventilation, while among the others who considered their ventilation sufficient, several had achieved this by adding hatches and/or fans after the start of the cruise. This aspect obviously should be dealt with at the designing or building stage, as boats meant for cruising in both temperate and tropical climates should have plenty of ventilation and hatches, ideally able to open both ways. That this can be a function of the design was pointed out by Hugh Brown, whose *Nightwing* was an open plan steel boat which allowed a free flow of air. This may not be easy to achieve with other construction materials.

The carrying capacity of a larger boat was another consideration mentioned by many of those interviewed, as stores, books and souvenirs always weigh more than designers allow for. Every smaller boat which had been away from base for longer than a year looked as though it was sinking under the added weight. Also, as some of these skippers pointed out, with a little more storage available, stores can be bought where they are cheapest. In these days of continuous inflation, when most boats start off on a long cruise with a fixed amount of money, it is often a wise investment to buy certain goods where and when they are conveniently priced. There are still a handful of ports around the world where one can buy most provisions and duty free liquor at knockdown prices, if one has the cash and space available.

DISPLACEMENT

The variety and range of cruising boats that I came across both in Suva and in later surveys prompted me to look more systematically at the factors that influence the choice of a boat. This I did in the Pacific survey, when I had the chance to ask questions left open in the previous surveys. How many people, for instance, seriously consider the displacement aspect before choosing a particular design, especially the ratio between displacement and ballast? In the most recent survey, just over half the skippers (26) told me that it was indeed a factor that they had considered before choosing their particular boat, even if not the prime consideration when it came to the final decision. It would appear that many people are still happy to leave this aspect to the designer, which may not always be wise as several of those interviewed admitted that they were unhappy with the displacement ratio of their boats. Two boats had to have ballast added as they were too light, while another four skippers regarded their boats as being overballasted, about which they could do very little, as in all cases the ballast was permanently encased. Several skippers repeated the observation made by some skippers in the Suva survey that designers should take into account the additional weight of fuel, water, stores and gear carried by the average cruising boat when calculating the total weight of the boat and the optimum ballast to be added.

Hull Form

The demand for more spaciousness has resulted in modern cruising boats being generally beamier and having more freeboard than older designs. In the Suva survey the ratio of beam to length was less for older boats. The overall ratio of beam to length on deck for the 57 monohulls was 30·8 per cent, being higher for the smaller sized boats.

Similar conclusions could be drawn in the case of draft, where as to be expected the larger the boat the deeper the draft. Although the skippers were not asked to rate the draft of their boats, a deeper draft was often mentioned as a disadvantage in certain cruising areas. This was one of the reasons why the majority had chosen a long keel rather than a fin keel, as boats fitted with the latter type of keel tend to draw more.

Among the 57 monohulls in Suva, 39 had a full keel, which was rated an average 9, a similar rating being awarded to the eight boats with a medium keel. The eight fin keelers received an average rating of 8·9, while two of the smaller boats with bilge keels were rated 6·5. Among the boats classified as long keelers, three had centreboards, which were not rated separately. However, in the Pacific survey, an equal number of centreboarders (3) rated this feature on average 7·5. Their owners explained that they had chosen a centreboard because they wanted a shallow draft boat, the lower average rating reflecting some dissatisfaction with the lowering and raising gear rather than with the centreboards themselves. In their cruising, they had all taken advantage of their draft. The crew of *Ondine*, for example, had explored the

Gambia river in Africa, the Oyapok in Brazil and had cruised extensively in the Everglades in Florida.

A shallow draft is one of the reasons why people choose a multihull, but it was remarkable that I did not come across any cruising multihulls when I gathered material for the Pacific survey. Just as in previous surveys, the most popular type of keel was the full keel, with 30 boats coming in this category. The full keel was rated an average 9·1, while the nine boats with a medium long keel were rated 8·2. The eight fin keeled boats received a higher average of 8·7; although their owners mentioned some disadvantages, such as the tendency of some fin keelers to sail their anchor in strong winds. The skippers of *Haubaut* and *Penelope*, both medium keelers, said that their boats lacked directional stability, tended to go into the wind easily and had too much weatherhelm.

The full keel has remained the most popular choice of long distance sailors, who consider it to be more suitable for ocean cruising and are prepared to sacrifice some speed in return for a sturdier underwater profile. Max Graveleau, an experienced Cape-Horner, now on his second world voyage on *Hispania*, summed up the full keel's popularity, saying, 'Sooner or later, if one cruises long enough, one is bound to hit something and this type of keel protects both the boat and the rudder.'

Beam, freeboard, hull shape and draft are all functions of the overall size of the boat and my general impression, after concluding the various surveys, was that most cruising people are less interested in the particular aspects of boat design than racing people are. They choose their boats for the overall aesthetic and functional design and are quite happy to leave the finer points of naval architecture to the designers. Perhaps cruising people should show more interest in boat design, for I feel that in recent years, too many racing features have crept into cruising boat design, which are not necessarily an improvement for cruising requirements. A case in point is the tendency to less and less protected rudders, some designers even dispensing with a skeg altogether.

General considerations similarly seem to dictate the choice of mono or multihull. Out of the 62 boats in the Suva survey, five were multihulls and the average rating given to their overall design was 7·8, as compared to the average rating of 8·6 given to the 57 monohulls. Generally multihulls do not appear to be so popular among the long distance voyagers, as many skippers still express serious reservations about the general safety of multihulls for this type of voyaging. It is certainly my opinion that the obvious advantages of multihulls, such as speed, spaciousness and moderate draft, do not make up for my doubts that even a well designed multihull may not stand up to the extreme conditions that one may encounter in long distance ocean voyaging.

The Rig

After the size and satisfaction with the general design of the boat, the question of rig was considered. In the Suva survey, exactly half of the boats were single-masted, generally the smaller ones. All the skippers were very firm in their assessment of the particular rig they carried and were precise in outlining its advantages or shortcomings. Overall, cutters received the highest ratings (see Table 2) and a number of sloop owners specified that they would have preferred a cutter to a sloop for extended cruising. Among the ketches, the twelve that were provided with a boomed staysail were rated higher by their owners (average rating 8·4), than the ketches without a staysail (7·9), most owners of the latter type stating that they would have preferred a staysail arrangement. Two boats were able to hoist a staysail on a provisional inner forestay, which could be moved back to the mast when not needed. As for the schooners, it was interesting to note that the rig was rated as low as 2 by a shorthanded skipper while, at the other extreme, a schooner with a crew of eight was rated the maximum 10. One disgruntled skipper, Miles Corener, who had built his *Sea Swan* from scratch with timber chosen and hewn out himself from the forests of Connecticut, was honest to admit, 'I only chose a schooner rig for its looks.' The third schooner was also rated highly by the skipper who used a square sail extensively, especially when shorthanded.

TABLE 2. *Comparison of rig, Suva and Pacific surveys.*

Rig	Suva Survey 1979			Pacific Survey 1984		
	No. of boats	Percentage of total	Average rating	No. of boats	Percentage of total	Average rating
Sloop	19	31%	8·6	19	38%	8·5
Cutter	12	19%	9·3	13	26%	9·2
Ketch	27	44%	8·1	15	30%	6·8
Yawl	1	1·5%	5	2	4%	10
Schooner	3	5%	7·3	1	2%	8
Total	62			50		

In the Cruising survey, cutters were equally popular, making up almost half of the one-masted boats. Again the two masted boats were generally the larger ones, there being twenty ketches, one schooner and one yawl. The dozen

The eyecatching schooner *Sea Swan* at anchor in Suva, designed and built by the owner Miles Corener with traditional beauty in mind.

successful circumnavigators, who on the whole sailed smaller than average boats, comprised eight sloops, one cutter, and three ketches. Three of the sloop owners did specify that their next boat would definitely be a cutter.

Similar conclusions can be drawn from the Pacific survey, in which two-thirds of the boats were singlemasted (32), the thirteen cutters receiving the highest average rating of 9·2, the nineteen sloops being rated an average 8·4. The fifteen ketches received the lowest rating of 6·8, although the eleven fitted with a staysail were rated higher than the four without. Generally, the owners of larger boats were in favour of a two masted configuration, pointing out that this had the advantage of a combination of smaller sails and also the use of mizzen on its own. Several skippers of boats under 40 ft admitted that initially they had thought that a ketch rig would make life easier in heavy weather, only to find later that they did not meet much heavy weather along the trade wind route and that their boats were slow and undercanvassed most of the time. To increase their sailing efficiency two boats had altered their fractional rig to masthead sloop, while on *Prospector* a yard had been added for downwind runs.

Rather than have a divided sail plan by a ketch arrangement, many skippers prefer to achieve this by means of a cutter. The simplicity and flexibility of a cutter rig was often stressed, especially by those who had sailed extensively on cutters before. Among the sloops in the Pacific survey, four had been altered to cutter en route, two by the addition of permanent stays, two by fitting removable stays.

The choice of rig for an offshore cruising boat is one of the most difficult decisions to be taken and many people leave it to the designer. Several skippers mentioned that the rig came with the boat and that they should have put more thought into this aspect. The most forthright critic was John Whitehead of *Cornelia* who said, 'Sailing literature gives the idea that for a boat over 40 ft two masts are essential. It is in fact totally wrong.'

The cutter *Runestaff* tacking past *Lou IV*, *Hägar* and *Rhodora* in Suva harbour. For long distance cruising, a cutter is regarded by most skippers as the most suitable rig.

Nevertheless, many of the larger boats in my various surveys were two masted as much for aesthetic as for practical reasons, especially those with an after cabin where the design appeared more balanced with a second mast. *Sea Swan*'s owner was not the only one who chose his boat for its looks.

Construction Material

As in the case of their rig, skippers were very precise when asked to give a rating to the construction material of their boat. Over half the boats in the Suva survey were of fibreglass, which received the average rating of 9. Metal boats were rated the highest, each of the five steel boats being rated 10, as was the only light alloy hull. As might be expected in tropical waters, the 19 wooden boats received a lower rating of 7·4, although in the few cases where the hull was sheathed in fibreglass, whether it was made from solid wood or plywood, the material attracted higher marks.

In the Pacific survey, the percentage of wooden boats remained the same, but there was a marked increase in the rating given to the 15 boats that came under the general heading of 'wood', including a variety of different

Ian Hancock of *Runestaff* is among the increasing number of long distance voyagers changing over to steel. In Whangarei he is putting the finishing touches to his 43 ft *Iron Butterfly*.

constructions from solid teak to plywood. Compared to the previous surveys, I was surprised to find wood being awarded a high average rating of 8·9. The owners of many of the wooden boats obviously had a very strong affection for this material, reflected in the very high ratings given by those who had built their boats themselves or the owners of older craft. These older boats certainly had more character than their modern synthetic counterparts. In contrast to this, owners of fibreglass boats took a more detached view and often gave a lower rating as soon as the first blisters appeared on their sorely tried hulls. It may be that the rash of blisters is an allergy to an overcritical owner!

Another tendency highlighted by the most recent survey was the gradual switchover to metal hulls, the proportion of steel boats having increased from 8 to 28 per cent. Many sailors who cruise among the reef infested waters of the South Pacific appear to feel safer on a steel boat and this explains the large increase in their numbers. It is a tendency that first came to light among the dozen circumnavigators interviewed, when several stated that they were planning to switch over to metal hulls for their next boat. Since then four of them have already done so and have left on a new voyage.

TABLE 3. *Comparison of construction material, Suva and Pacific surveys.*

Material	Suva Survey 1979			Pacific Survey 1984		
	No. of boats	Percentage of total	Average rating	No. of boats	Percentage of total	Average rating
GRP	33	53%	9	20	40%	8·1
Wood	19	31%	7·4	15	30%	8·9
Steel	5	8%	10	14	28%	8·6
Light alloy	1	1·5%	10	1	2%	9
Ferro-cement	4	6.5%	9	—	—	—
Total	62			50		

Conclusion

In spite of various shortcomings and faults that came to light during my lengthy discussions with the skippers during the Pacific survey, more of them expressed a general satisfaction with their choice of boat than did the 62 skippers I interviewed in Suva six years earlier. Only thirteen skippers had bought their boats new, while twenty of the boats had been bought second hand, four of these being pre-war, with the oldest among them, *Pytheas*, a Dutch Pilot cutter, being at least eighty years old, and *Moli*, a Colin Archer type design, had been built in Norway in 1918. The remaining boats were built by their owners, fourteen from scratch and three fitting out professionally built hulls (*Atair II*, *Ondine*, and *Madame Bertrand*). Maybe *Moon River* should be included in the own-built category as this 1937 Carl Albert designed boat was purchased as a wreck and totally rebuilt by its present owners, Bob and Nancy Pihl.

When asked why they had chosen their particular boats, several skippers used the expression 'love at first sight', which can only mean that outward appearances still play an important role in the choice of a boat. Other skippers mentioned that they chose their boats primarily for comfort and that they were prepared to accept a heavier displacement as a trade-off for speed. The owners of the three centreboard boats chose them expressly for their shallow draft, which they considered essential for their particular cruising plans. Twelve skippers chose their boats because the price was right, and as to be expected these were mostly among those buying second hand. Many of these knew exactly what they were looking for and often ended up with a bargain, purchasing a well equipped and sea-tried boat. On the other hand, over half the skippers (27) made their particular choice because the boat in question was 'nearest to their ideal cruising boat'.

Obviously among such a variety of boats, people chose their craft for different reasons and 'ideal' had many meanings. For Fearon Anderson, the chance to buy an International 12 metre boat like *Chanceeggar*, built as the French entry for the 1972 Americas Cup, was the fulfilment of a lifetime dream. Sailing *Chanceeggar* the 14,000 miles from England to New Zealand virtually singlehanded had not changed his opinion of the boat – according to him it was the only 12 metre boat ever built capable of cruising safely offshore. At the other end of the scale was Mike Bailes, after 20 years of sailing over 100,000 miles in his Folkboat *Jellicle*, still giving it top marks of 10 as his ideal boat. Eduard van Zelderen showed his satisfaction in his own built *White Pointer*, by setting off on a second world voyage with his family not long after completing their first circumnavigation.

Some of the skippers who had built their own boats chose a particular design for ease of construction. Foremost among these was Hugh Brown, who built and fitted out *Nightwing* in only one year. The average time taken by the home builders was nearly three years. Several of these builders had a definite affection for their boats, while freely admitting some of their faults. Serge Veuve, who spent five years building his steel *Penelope* in Switzerland, put it well, saying, 'Like a woman you love, you excuse her faults.'

Nevertheless, every skipper was asked to point out any major drawbacks in the design of his boat. Thirty expressed general satisfaction and had no criticism to make. The most common cause for complaint was the slowness in light airs and poor windward capabilities of some of the boats, only to be expected from solidly built, heavy displacement boats laden with gear and stores. Other drawbacks mentioned were excessive weatherhelm, too deep a draft, too much maintenance on older steel boats, or poor access to the engine and batteries even to carry out routine work.

Several people tried to rectify these drawbacks, sometimes carrying out major modifications en route. Besides those changing to a more efficient rig, *Ave del Mar* had her bowsprit lengthened and her mast raked forward to correct an excessive weatherhelm. The skipper of *Haubaut* was hoping to reduce weatherhelm by the addition of a skirt on the stern, which would also act as a convenient swimming and diving platform. This modification had already been carried out on *El Djezair*, whose skipper stressed its advantage as a safety factor, allowing easy access back on board, especially on boats with a high freeboard.

Two skippers were planning to restep their masts from the deck to the keel, which they considered safer for extended cruising, while another two were planning to change their heavy wooden spars to light alloy. *Spirit of Cockpit* had already carried out this modification to aluminium spars, changing also from galvanised to stainless steel rigging, as had *White Pointer*. Three ex-racing boats had been gradually converted to be more suitable for cruising, mainly by introducing measures of comfort and safety. *Spray* had her rudder strengthened after losing most of the original one following a collision with an unidentified object off Martinique, subsequently moving the sacrificial point lower down to retain more of the rudder in case of another collision. The addition of washboards to the main companionway of *Keegenoo* was pointed out as a safety feature lacking in the original design.

When looking at the skippers' overall satisfaction with their particular boats, it was interesting to note that the 27 skippers who had originally chosen their boats for being nearest to their ideal boat were comparatively less contented with their choice, giving them an average rating of only 8·3 as compared to the general rating of 9. Many admitted that experience had taught them a lot and this would greatly influence any future choice. I therefore probed further into this by asking each skipper to describe his ideal boat for a hypothetical future voyage, but keeping within realistic bounds.

Among the 48 skippers in the Pacific survey who would consider such a voyage again, nine were perfectly happy with their present boat and would not change them even if they had the choice. 26 skippers would opt for the same size as their present boat, four would prefer smaller boats, while 20 would go for something slightly larger. The overall tendency towards metal boats was reinforced when half the skippers said they would prefer steel or light alloy for their ideal boat, one third would opt for fibreglass and the remaining nine would choose wood again.

A similar tendency was shown in the choice of rig, with 80 per cent of the skippers expressing a preference for a single masted rig. Among these, the majority would choose a cutter or a sloop with a removable inner stay. The other 20 per cent who would prefer two masts, whether ketch, yawl or schooner, were thinking of larger boats for their ideal. Two skippers explained that the only reason they would choose a ketch or yawl was the convenience offered by the mizzen mast for mounting a radar scanner.

The optimum size of an ocean cruising boat has often been debated, and in the Pacific survey the average length was 38 ft overall, which is very close to the mean of previous cruising surveys. In fact over half of the boats were in the 35–45 ft range. This confirms a personal observation that there has been a move from the extremes towards the middle ground, the number of very large or very small boats cruising offshore having declined in recent years. Why this should have happened is difficult to say, although in the case of the larger boats the difficulty of finding competent and compatible crews for long ocean passages may have something to do with it. The cost of maintaining and running a very large boat may also be another explanation. Many skippers prefer to have a boat that they can sail shorthanded if necessary. At the other extreme, it has already been proven that it is possible to cross oceans in very small craft, so fewer people are prepared to set off in a small boat just to make a point, and prefer to buy a larger, more comfortable boat. The large selection of second-hand boats on the market means that even people with limited funds are not necesarily restricted to a smaller boat. The proliferation of medium size boats has also been influenced by the fact that cruising nowadays is mainly a family affair. The vast majority of boats in the survey were crewed by couples, either on their own or with their children.

These are some of the reasons why the most contented group in the Pacific survey were those owning boats in the 30–40 ft range, these 27 skippers giving their boats an average rating of 9.1. A lower rating of 7.4 given by the 22 owners of craft over 40 ft shows perhaps that choosing the largest boat one can afford is not always the best idea.

Talking to so many skippers over the years and listening to countless descriptions of 'ideal' boats, the only conclusion I can draw is that whatever boat one chooses, what matters most is the determination to go. These surveys confirmed my belief that many people set off in whatever boat they happen to own at the time, ideal or not. The motley collection of boats one meets sailing the oceans of the world may not be the ideal cruising boats, but their owners are the ones getting on with the cruising, not just dreaming or talking about it. For these crews the dream of cruising to faraway places has become reality.

One Excellent Boat – Hägar the Horrible

Only a handful of the boats I met in Suva came close to matching the ideals which emerged from my survey, although there was one outstanding example, which fulfilled virtually all the criteria of a perfect cruising boat. This was *Hägar the Horrible*, a 40 ft steel cutter from Sydney. Both on deck and below she was simple and functional. Her owner, Gunter Gross, had built her himself from a slightly modified design by the Australian designer Joe Adams.

A steel hull seemed the obvious choice for a boat built to cruise extensively the reef strewn waters of the South Pacific. The high ratings given to metal as

The steel cutter *Hägar the Horrible* from Sydney sailing out of Port Vila in the New Hebrides.

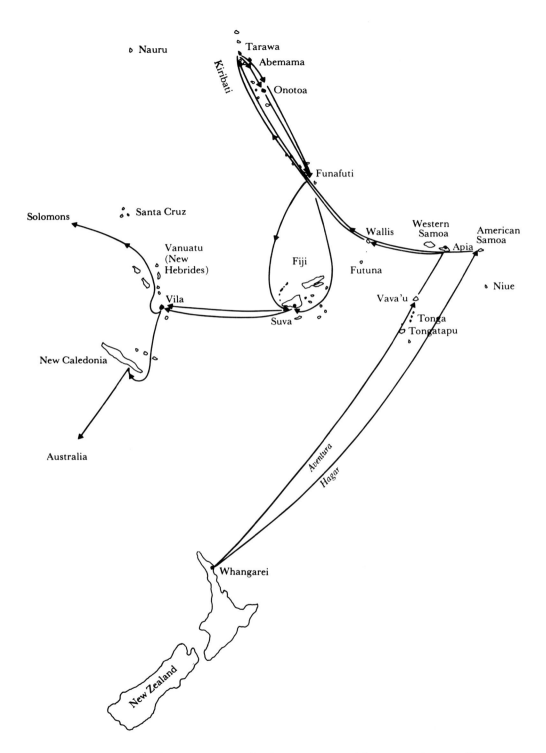

MAP B Track of *Aventura*'s cruise in company with *Hägar the Horrible*

a construction material reflected the confidence associated with the strength of a metal hull. As all those who have sailed for any length of time in reef areas know only too well, however careful they are, sooner or later they may tangle with some coral heads. From this point of view alone, a metal hull has certain advantages over other materials. Being aware of the shortcomings of steel, Gunter had taken every conceivable precaution during construction to avoid any places where moisture could be trapped and cause rusting. The entire hull was easily inspected from inside by removable floorboards and an ingenious modular furniture held in place by bolts. The steel was properly prepared and painted from the beginning.

Although of a fairly high aspect ratio, *Hägar* is easy to handle due to her cutter rig arrangement, with a selftending staysail controlled by a wishbone frame. The multichine hull is easily driven and performed well on all points of sailing, as I know only too well, being always left far behind whenever *Hägar* and my own *Aventura* sailed in company.

Gunter is an adventurer in the true sense of the word, something he proved the day I mentioned my intention to sail from New Zealand to the Independence celebrations in Tarawa, the island capital of the Gilbert Islands. We had spent the cyclone season together in Whangarei and although Gunter was planning soon to set sail for Tahiti once again, he changed his plans on the spot, undaunted by a detour of over 2,000 miles just to join in the festivities.

Although now Australian, Gunter was born in Germany and trained as a chef. Working on the Holland American Line he became convinced that sailing was his life, so with his excellent qualification he roamed the globe, trying to put enough money together to finance the boat of his dreams. From charter boats in the Caribbean to lumber camps in Canada and managing swish hotels in South Africa, it was finally as a cook at a bauxite mine in Australia that Gunter got enough cash together to have a 34 ft steel hull built, which he fitted out himself. Cruising up the Barrier reef, he soon found it was not a perfect blue water boat, so he decided to set about building the perfect boat with his own hands. Two years of hard work produced *Hägar the Horrible*.

Roving adventurer he may be, but Gunter is a meticulous skipper and his boat is always in tip top condition. He maintains his boat as he goes along, not allowing any job to be too long postponed. Six years of cruising have taken him 30,000 miles back and forth across the Pacific and he has realised his dream of making sailing his life. When he needs more money he stops to work, but one is more likely to find him as a boilermaker than a chef these days, as he has grown to enjoy working with metal as a medium. Although he usually has friends or crew on board, Gunter does sail *Hägar* singlehanded from time to time. I have certainly been impressed with the ease with which she handles and after spending several months in *Hägar's* company, the boat certainly gets my vote as one of the nearest to perfect among the cruising boats I surveyed.

Gunter Gross always keeps *Hägar* in good condition by doing maintenance work as it arises.

CHAPTER TWO

Equipment and Instrumentation

A well designed and strongly built boat is the first priority for most people preparing for an ocean voyage, but when it comes to the choice of equipment, an order of priorities is more difficult to establish. The range available is enormous and choosing the best not a simple matter, for a disturbing proportion of the equipment on the market is of poor quality, unable to stand up to the treatment that is inevitable on boats sailing thousands of miles every year.

Undoubtedly the best testing ground for cruising equipment is the ocean and any weaknesses or faults will soon show up under the gruelling conditions of a long passage. In order to revise the information obtained in my previous surveys, and also to find out more about how modern equipment was faring on sailing boats, I returned to the Pacific to carry out a comprehensive study of gear and instruments.

The fifty skippers whom I interviewed in various ports from Tahiti to New Zealand had all sailed a minimum of 10,000 miles or had spent at least one year full-time cruising. In fact, most exceeded these criteria, several already having completed a circumnavigation, while for others cruising was their way of life. The average sailing experience per skipper came to over 23 years and the number of miles sailed on just the present voyage averaged at nearly 25,000 miles per boat, many skippers having made extensive previous voyages.

The survey dealt with many issues and brought to light a wealth of interesting material, sometimes confirming and sometimes contradicting earlier findings. Among the fifty boats, the amount of equipment failure was considerable, my general impression being that much of the equipment labelled 'marine' should never have been allowed to come anywhere near the sea.

Sails

The number and type of sails carried by the 50 boats in the Pacific survey varied enormously, some carrying a complete second suit of sails, with 20 boats in the sample having a spare mainsail on board. 25 boats had a trisail for strong winds, some trisails being kept permanently bagged at the bottom of the main mast, ready to be hoisted on a separate track. On some boats without a trisail, the skippers prefer to use a deeply reefed mainsail instead, while two ketch owners do away with the mainsail altogether in strong winds, using the mizzen with a storm jib. 43 boats had a storm jib, although these were not counted in the total number of foresails carried, which worked out at an average of nearly four sails per boat. Ten boats had twin jibs specially made for running in the trades and this arrangement received an average rating of 7·3. 18 boats had a spinnaker on board although they received an average rating of only 6·3 when their owners were asked to rate the spinnaker as a cruising sail. A higher average rating was given by the ten skippers who had cruising chutes, five boats giving it the maximum 10. The ratings given to both the chute and the spinnaker seemed to reflect the personal manner of sailing of individual skippers, having both devotees and detractors. The main criticism of these sails was that most boats could not be left to selfsteer while the sail was in use.

It was virtually the same conclusion that I had drawn during the Suva survey, when the subject of downwind sailing was discussed at length with the

Local boats racing in the Bay of Islands, a perfect place to spend the summer during the tropical cyclone season.

skippers, as many of them had sailed considerable distances under trade wind conditions. Among the 62 boats in the Suva survey, sixteen had twin jibs and/or genoas and every one of their skippers swore by them. Some of the twins were set flying or on the same stay with hanks alternating, although a few boats had twin forestays for this very reason. Some skippers mentioned that poled out twin jibs were easier on their self-steering, enabling it to be better balanced and work less, especially when running with a heavy following sea. For running downwind, two of the schooners used a square sail set on a yard, generally in winds of over twenty knots.

The wear and tear of cruising sails was examined in the Circumnavigators survey. Several boats replaced sails en route, usually the main and genoa, and their estimated mileage per sail worked out at an average of 30,000 miles, although this does not mean that the particular sail was actually used for all those miles. Of course the state of the sails on setting out was a critical factor, but a few boats completed their circumnavigations with all the same sails that they had set off with, including *Lou IV* who, with 46,000 miles in 4½ years, had made one of the longest voyages on one suit of seven sails.

The longevity of the sails depends on two main factors. First, the quality of the material and workmanship, and secondly the care taken looking after the sails. Continuous exposure to the tropical sun exerts a heavy toll on any sail, although certain brands and colours of synthetic materials appear to be more resistant to heat and ultraviolet rays than others. More often than not it is the stitching that disintegrates long before the material itself, and several boats had their sails restitched in New Zealand halfway through their voyage. Another boat which completed her 50,000 mile world voyage, virtually with all her original sails, even if repeatedly repaired, was the French yawl *Calao*. Her skipper, Erick Bouteleux, preferred to have his sails made from much heavier cloth than that usually recommended by sailmakers. *Calao*'s heavy sails stood up very well to six years of continuous cruising, even if Erick had to fall back on his 1000 sq ft spinnaker and mizzen staysail whenever the winds got too light.

Taking good care of sails can undoubtedly prolong their lives considerably. Herbert and Ilse Gieseking of *Lou IV*, who returned home with the same sails they had set out with, were always meticulous about putting on the sail covers the minute they dropped anchor, folding away carefully the sails which were not in use and giving all sails a rinse ashore with fresh water whenever possible.

Despite careful attention and good materials, sails will eventually wear out and it is only the lucky few who manage to arrive home after a world cruise with their original sails. When sails need replacing during a cruise, there are three options open to the skipper, to have new sails made locally, to order them elsewhere and fly them in, or to make the sails himself. Although a number of cruising boats carry a sewing machine on board, these are rarely used for actual sailmaking, but rather for sail repairs, the making of awnings and dodgers, loose covers, etc. Sailmaking is one of the few jobs which cruising people prefer to leave to the professionals.

With the world wide expansion of boating and sailing, there are now sailmakers to be found in all major centres along the cruising routes of the world. New Zealand and Australia are two countries where the sails made locally are of the same standard as those made in Europe and North America, in fact some of the old established sailmakers have their own branches in these countries. Hong Kong has also gained an international reputation for sailmaking of a good quality at a reasonable price and there are several sailmakers who are prompt at dispatching sails to every part of the globe. Some skippers still prefer to have their sails made by their original lofts, especially as these lofts usually hold sail plans, which makes ordering easier. The sailmaker will generally arrange the air freighting or shipping of the finished sails. In most countries, if the shipment is marked *In Transit*, the owner can redeem them from Customs without paying duty. This may have to be arranged through a local shipping agent. However in a few countries, goods cannot be imported duty free and the skipper would be well advised to make his enquiries at Customs before placing an order overseas. It is also worth choosing a port convenient to an international airport as, in some countries, Customs insist that the goods are accompanied by an officer until they are on board. These general points apply also to the import of any replacement parts for a cruising boat.

JIB FURLING

The number of boats fitted with jib furling has been steadily increasing in recent years, due both to the improvement of the gear and to its acceptance by the sailing community. Twelve boats in the Pacific survey had jib furling, three having added their gear en route, while a further five boats were in the process of adding jib furling or planned to do so in the near future. The average rating given to this gear by the twelve owners was 9, although the skippers gave a lower average of 8 when considering it as a means of reefing as opposed to furling. Some pertinent observations were also made by skippers on the use of the furling gear for reefing the jib.

The gears which are independent of the rigging and can be easily taken down were praised by their owners, such as singlehander Ted Judd of *Grendel*, who prefers to lower the gear in impending heavy weather. He prefers to use it only for running and broad reaching, especially at night.

Christian Gain makes an adjustment to his jib furling gear while *Spe-Ow* is sailing in Raiatea lagoon.

Juan Ribas of *Abuelo III* regards the gear as positively dangerous in heavy weather, as he nearly lost his mast in a storm when the furled up jib pulled away his masthead fitting. The weight of the gear, its windage and the violent motion of the boat in a short swell combined to produce a seesawing effect of such force that the entire masthead fitting was wrenched off the mast.

Another situation where jib furling gear proved to be a hazard was pointed out by two skippers who had witnessed the havoc wreaked by cyclones *Veena* and *Reva* in Tahiti in 1983, when scores of boats were driven ashore. On some boats the strong wind caught the exposed corner of the sail and forced it to unfurl, spelling disaster for the boats in question.

Although nine skippers did use the gear for reefing fairly often, some of them pointed out its shortcomings when trying to reduce sail area in this way. When the wind increases, one is left with a bulging roll on the luff and the clew high up in the air. The cut of the sail was obviously a crucial factor, while efficiency was improved by some skippers by moving the sheeting block on deck.

On the whole, however, most people appeared to use the system for furling rather that reefing. In strong winds they usually preferred to use smaller sails, in some cases hanked on a separate stay. In spite of these reservations, most skippers considered jib furling a bonus provided it was used properly. Heinz Hermanns of *Dumeklemmer II* had fitted jib furling type gear on all his sails, including main and mizzen, prior to setting off on his second circumnavigation.

HALYARDS

Whether to bring back all halyards to the cockpit or not is a matter of personal preference, especially as the increasing use of jib furling gear has reduced work on the foredeck to the minimum. In the Pacific survey only two boats had their halyards led back to the cockpit, while one had only the jib halyards brought back. Among the remaining 47, when questioned about the convenience of having all halyards in the cockpit, only four skippers thought it might be worth considering, all others being contented with their halyards at the foot of the mast. Joe McKeown of *Shanachie* had increased safety by mounting his halyard winches on deck at the foot of the mast. Also, as a means of making work on deck safer, three boats had mast pulpits, an arrangement praised by their owners.

Engines

The wind has long ceased to be the only energy source used in cruising and most boats I came across had auxiliary engines. All of the circumnavigators had inboard diesel engines, but these were generally little used except when entering and leaving port or motoring in the calmest of weathers. The majority of these twelve skippers estimated that they had sailed 95 per cent of the time. Some of the smaller boats claimed to use their engines even less than this.

In the Cruising survey, only three out of fifty boats were engineless. This was by deliberate choice, although Albert Steele later fitted an engine in his *Peregrine*, for the sole purpose of pottering among the reef-infested waters of the Tongan archipelago.

In my Suva survey, two boats were engineless, also by choice, although both skippers agreed that life would have been easier *with* an engine. In this survey I asked for more details about the engines, and requested a rating. Of the sixty boats with engines, the two smallest boats had outboard motors, one boat had a petrol (gasoline) inboard engine, rated 0, and the remaining fifty-seven were all equipped with diesel engines. The overall reliability of the diesel engines was shown by the average rating of 8·8. Nevertheless, some makes were rated higher than others. This did not necessarily reflect the better quality of the engine in question, but often the availability of spare parts and the ease of getting repairs dealt with promptly.

Several owners complained at the difficulty of finding parts for their Volvo engines in the Pacific, and this complaint was borne out by the low rating of 7 given to the twelve Volvo engines surveyed. The eighteen Perkins engines (14 Perkins, 4 Westerbeke) received a better average rating of 9·5. Parts for these engines are relatively easy to find, as in many cases the same parts are used in heavy plant or truck engines, and these are available in most countries. For similar reasons, the five Ford engines were also rated high at an average of 8·9.

A similar pattern emerged from the Pacific survey in which 48 boats had engines, only *Madame Bertrand* and *Jellicle* being engineless. The most common make was again Perkins, the 18 owners (15 Perkins, 3 Westerbeke) rating them an average 8·7. The same average rating was given to the six Yanmars, while the three Fords in the sample received 8·8. The lowest average rating of 5·8 was given to the five Volvo engines, although Paul Benoidt of *Ondine* pointed out that the main engine was perhaps not so much to blame as the auxiliary equipment on it (alternator, starter motor, pumps, etc.). Volvos were also rated poorly when the skippers were asked to give their opinion on the availability of engine parts worldwide. 16 of the Perkins owners said that finding parts was easy, two skippers (*Barfly* and *Spirit of Cockpit*) having specifically chosen Perkins engines for this reason. Yanmar and Ford were the other makes for which parts appeared to be found without difficulty. The few Saabs, Bukhs and Ferrymans, although rated high by their owners, have the disadvantage shared with other less common makes in not having an extensive international network of agents. Because of this some of the owners of less common makes had the foresight to carry a selection of spares with them. The minimum specified by various skippers included a head gasket, at least one complete injector, a belt for the alternator and impellers for the various pumps. Equally important was the recommended set of tools for the engine in question, a workshop manual and a diagram showing all part numbers.

ENGINE SIZE

For cruising in Pacific waters most skippers were of the opinion that a sufficiently powerful engine was essential. Many passes into lagoons have strong outflowing currents, being on the leeward side of the islands; and a lot of them are too narrow for tacking. Although engine power was discussed in my earlier surveys, in the Pacific survey I tried to examine this subject in more detail. Every skipper was asked if his engine was powerful enough for the size of boat and the particular requirements of his cruise. 31 skippers thought that they had adequate power, five that their engines were more powerful than necessary, while twelve skippers thought their engines were not powerful enough. The power rating per boat came to an average of 40 HP, which I consider to be a realistic figure for the average length of 38 ft. Looking more closely at the twelve boats considered underpowered, their average length was 37 ft, while their average engine rating was just under 24 HP per boat. This prompted me to conclude that, as in my previous cruising survey, a good rule of thumb is to allow 1 HP per foot length of boat.

Fuel capacity and range under power were also discussed, the boats carrying on average 90 gallons of fuel in their tanks, although several skippers took on extra fuel in jerrycans for longer passages or when cruising in areas where diesel fuel was not readily available. The average range under power when motoring in calm conditions was 750 miles per boat or an average consumption of 0·4 gallons per hour.

On the whole skippers had encountered fewer problems with their engines than those interviewed in my previous surveys, many emphasising that they had never needed to find out if spare parts were available or not. Nevertheless Max Fletcher of *Christopher Robin* stressed that the reason why diesel engines gave more trouble on sailing boats was because far too often they were not run under load – perhaps only to charge up batteries or to leave or enter anchorage under low revs.

Generators

The generating of electricity seemed to be a matter of serious concern for these long distance sailors, for 26 boats carried generators, six of them fixed and twenty being portable. There were also five wind generators, usually rigged up only in port, three towing generators and two alternators mounted on the freewheeling propshaft. Robert Lowe of *Windrace*, who had his alternator specially installed to run a fridge while underway, complained that it only cut in at about 4·5 knots and that a lower cut-in speed would have given the crew a chance to have a cold drink also when the boat was sailing slowly.

The advent of solar panels (photovoltaic cells) is one of the striking changes that have occurred in long distance cruising in the last few years. 23 boats had one or more solar panels, most of them acquired at a very reasonable price in

Juan Ribas demonstrates how his solar panels are rigged up on *Abuelo III*.

Tahiti, where the development of renewable energy sources is heavily subsidised. Some boats had four, five or even six panels on board, although only one or two were used at sea and the rest rigged up during longer stays in port. All their users were very happy with this way of charging their batteries, an average panel providing at least 12 amps per day.

BATTERIES

The average number of batteries was three per boat with an average capacity of 135 Ah. The majority of boats had two batteries for general consumption, usually of larger capacity, and a separate one of 60 – 100 Ah kept for engine starting only. Solar panels have simplified matters greatly and, especially on boats with a moderate consumption of electricity, one or two panels rated at 36 W each gave a steady supply of current covering most needs. On two boats the panels were kept as an emergency back-up and were stowed away to be used only if the other systems failed. Solar power was used to provide electricity on engineless *Madame Bertrand*, which carried a 100 amp battery charged by a 36 W photovoltaic cell.

Provisioning and Refrigeration

In the Suva survey less than half the boats (45 per cent) had refrigeration of some kind. Those fitted with a mechanical compressor were rated the highest at 9·4, while those with an electrical compressor were rated at 7·7, those running on paraffin (kerosene) at 7·5 and those on bottled gas at 6·3. In the case of freezers, the seventeen boats that had them (27 per cent of the total) rated those driven by mechanical compressors much higher at 9·3, than those with electrical compressors, rated 6·3. Generally, I found that a mechanical compressor attached to the main engine gave by far the best results and attracted the highest ratings from their users, as it supplied both the freezer and the fridge. On boats with electrical refrigeration, the main engine had to be run for approximately forty-five minutes to one hour a day, with the added advantage of the batteries being charged at the same time.

These findings were confirmed by the Pacific survey in which 17 boats had an electric refrigerator, two of them the combined type that also runs on gas if required, while four worked in conjunction with freezers which were fitted with an electric compressor. Several fridges were used only in port either because they consumed too much electricity or because they did not function properly when the boat was in constant motion. For the same reason the three gas fridges were not used at sea. The four electric freezers seemed to give less satisfaction and were rated only 7·5, compared to the average rating of 9·3 given to the nine freezers operated by mechanical compressors run off the main engine.

In spite of the general improvement in refrigeration equipment, many voyagers still prefer to do without, mainly because of the daily chore of running the engine or generator. Instead of stocking up with frozen stores, many prefer to do their own canning. This subject was investigated also in the Pacific survey, when I was told that 26 skippers, or more usually their mates, preserved their own food in one way or another, mostly by canning or bottling in their pressure cookers a variety of meats, fish, fruit and vegetables. The plentifulness of fruit was often taken advantage of to make jams or preserves. Excess fish caught were dealt with in a variety of ways from freezing to pickling, salting or drying. In most cases a pressure cooker was used for canning, 45 boats having at least one pressure cooker on board, several having two or even three and emphasising their usefulness on a boat. Hugh Brown of *Nightwing* carried a pressure canner instead of a pressure cooker, with which he had canned a whole range of food. The importance of having a gauge on a pressure cooker was pointed out by one skipper who had suffered from food poisoning caused by poorly canned meat.

For long term storage, tinned foods made up the largest proportion of the stores carried by 19 of the boats, whereas twelve preferred to carry more dried or freeze-dried goods. The remaining boats kept a balanced mixture of all types of stores, a few making a special effort to use as much fresh food as possible. Only one boat relied on the freezer for the bulk of its stores, while another reminded me that some countries, Australia particularly, confiscate all frozen meats on board. Another skipper no longer keeps his stores this way after losing 120 kg of meat when his freezer broke down.

The usual length of time that people provisioned for was from 3 to 6 months (25 boats), only seven provisioning for as long as a year and two for less than 6 weeks. Several crews planned only for a particular passage or else calculated for twice or three times the intended length of the voyage. Some skippers bought larger quantities in countries where the goods were cheaper or of better quality.

FRESH WATER CAPACITY

The average amount of fresh water carried by the fifty boats was 105 gallons. This capacity was adequate for the vast majority of those interviewed, only a few carrying additional jerrycans on deck, mostly on boats with smaller than average built-in tanks. In some cases jerrycans of water were kept on deck as part of the skipper's precautions in case of abandoning ship.

Sixteen boats had a pressurised water system, although a few skippers specified that they preferred to pump the water manually on passage and only use the pressure system where there was plenty of water available. On twelve boats the system also provided hot water, while twenty boats had a fixed shower installed. An additional number had a portable deck shower, often used in conjunction with special water bags. These black plastic bags containing about 2 gallons of water are left in the sun as a very efficient means of providing hot water. On *Northern Chinook*, the hot water was poured into a large insecticide sprayer mounted in the shower room, which was an ingenious way of providing a pressurised hot shower without the use of electricity.

COOKING FUEL

Bottled gas, propane or butane, remains the most popular cooking fuel, 27 boats using it and giving it an average rating of 9·3, several skippers making the proviso of observing certain safety rules.

The 24 boats using paraffin (kerosene) stoves were less contented, giving

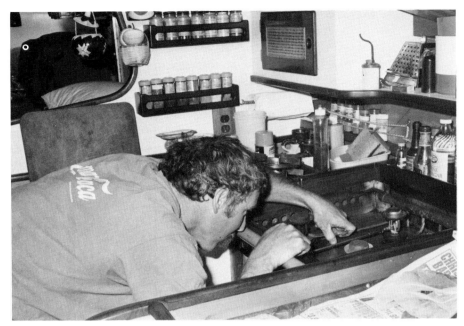

Joe McKeown of *Shanachie* converting two of his kerosene burners to gas.

them an average rating of 7·4, one skipper specifically stating that it was dangerous lighting his paraffin stove in a seaway. Three boats had recently changed from paraffin to gas while on another boat the skipper was planning to convert two of his burners to gas because of the problems his crew had encountered using the paraffin burners.

Two boats cooked with 220 V electricity and both rated this system the maximum 10, even if it meant starting the generator every time they wanted to cook. They both also had a paraffin stove on board as a standby. One crew cooked with methylated spirit, which it rated 5.

Most crews had no problems filling their gas bottles, although the type of fitting on the bottles varies between countries, some European systems being difficult to fill in New Zealand or the United States. Venezuela and the North West Pacific were other areas mentioned where difficulties were encountered. Problems were also met in the Mediterranean by boats equipped with non-European type containers. Unfortunately these have not been standardised internationally and valve fittings often vary from country to country. Some cautious skippers carry the necessary adapters with them, as many filling stations do not have them.

The containers can be used for either propane or butane, propane being the fuel more generally available in tropical countries, but this can cause damage to burners on cookers designed for use with butane gas. These burners tend to burn out and have to be replaced more frequently. When changing from propane to butane, which is used in temperate countries, it is wise to change the regulator or have its rating checked. The average consumption of gas on most cruising boats was less than 10 lb per month.

Instrumentation

The unprecedented advance in electronics in recent years has enabled cruising boats to carry an entire range of the latest instruments, powerful radios, radar and satellite navigation equipment. In spite of the proliferation of electronic instruments, many of the sailors I encountered chose to navigate in the traditional manner as part of their general philosophy and relationship with the sea.

One of the primary aims of the Pacific survey was to examine the impact of electronics on small boat navigation. Nevertheless, before investigating electronic instruments, of which some were found even on modestly equipped boats, I tried to find out how much use the skippers had for the classic instruments of navigation. Every single boat carried at least one sextant, many also having a standby sextant, usually of the plastic type. Every boat except one had a handbearing compass for coastal navigation, while 41 carried a leadline, even if (as in most cases) they had a depth sounder as well. 31 boats had a mechanical log, generally of the trailing type. 47 boats had a barometer, while nine had a barograph as well as or instead of the barometer, only one boat having neither, a surprising omission on a boat that otherwise had a whole range of electronic gear.

Four purists navigated with compass, sextant and leadline only, these experienced skippers saying that they had no need for anything more than these basic instruments. In fact another six skippers also relied on classic instruments alone, with the addition of a taff rail log or depth sounder. One outspoken traditionalist among these was Einar Einarsson, who dismissed the usefulness of electronic instruments by saying, 'What was good enough for Captain Cook is good enough for me.' Indeed, on his *Irma* there were no electronics to be seen and all navigation was carried out by traditional methods.

ELECTRONIC INSTRUMENTS

Even among traditionalists, at least one electronic instrument was found on board the majority of boats, most commonly a depth sounder, 42 boats having

TABLE 4. *Incidence of electronic instruments in Pacific survey.*

Weatherfacsimile
Loran C
SSB radio
Computer
Wind direction
Wind speed
Radar
Amateur radio
EPIRB
SatNav
Speedometer/log
RDF
VHF radio
Depth sounder

No. of boats having each instrument

one and three of them having two. Their owners assessed the reliability and performance of these instruments with an average rating of 7·6. It was difficult to compare brands as there were 16 different makes, although the most commonly found was Seafarer on fifteen boats, which was also rated on average 7·6.

Over half the boats (28) had an electronic log, usually combined with a speedometer, attracting an average rating of 6·5 from the fifteen different makes, several of which performed quite poorly.

Only eleven boats had functioning wind speed indicators, which were rated on average 6·8. Several other skippers mentioned they had broken indicators, which they declined to rate. The situation was similar in the case of wind direction, the average rating of the eight units still working being 7·5. Four of these were part of integrated systems, whose skippers were satisfied, giving these systems an average rating of 9.

32 boats had RDF and the 25 skippers who rated their RDF sets gave it an average of 7·3. The most common among the fifteen makes were Sailor, the six sets receiving a rating of 8·1, and Seafix, the five sets being rated on average 6. Seven of the skippers did not rate RDF as they had never or very rarely used this equipment, often pointing out that the lack of beacons in the South Pacific rendered it useless.

On eight boats a navigational computer was used for various calculations in astro-navigation. The five different makes were highly rated by their owners, who described these intruments as very handy and extremely useful. One skipper used the computer to store various data, such as the call signs of the many radio amateurs he was in contact with. The more advanced of these computers not only stored data found in the *Nautical Almanac* for several years to come, but could also be used by their owners to write their personal navigational programs.

Two boats were equipped with Loran C and both of them rated it 10 for areas where it was available, but 0 for the Pacific. Probably for a similar reason no boats had Omega or Decca navigational systems.

This lack of navigational aids in the Pacific explains the popularity of SatNavs among today's Pacific navigators. Since my last survey there has been a dramatic increase in their number, over half of the boats (27) in the Pacific survey using satellite navigation. As the advent of SatNav appears to have revolutionised many people's approach to offshore navigation, I used this opportunity to examine closely the use of this particular piece of equipment.

The seven different makes of SatNavs attracted an average rating of 8·2. The commonest were the three models of Walker, which were given an average rating of 6·9 by their nine owners, some of whom complained about the unreliability of this make and poor after-sales service. The six owners of

Shipmate SatNavs gave them an average rating of 8·5, while the five owners of Magnavox rated their equipment on average 9.

The skippers were also asked their opinion about having satellite navigation and practically every one of them agreed that it was extremely useful. Nevertheless when I asked them if they considered this equipment to be *essential* on a cruising boat, 19 skippers replied in the negative, only seven skippers regarding their SatNavs as essential, three of them pointing out that it was their insurance policy.

Paul Benoidt of *Ondine*, an ex-naval captain, said, 'SatNav is only essential if you choose to sail to difficult places.' Having sailed half way round the world without one, he purchased his SatNav specifically to sail in the Tuamotu archipelago.

That SatNavs can be very useful was shown by the fact that 15 skippers used theirs all the time, the rest using it irregularly, while four skippers, who still preferred to navigate by traditional methods, only used their SatNavs when approaching land or when there was no sun.

The skippers were also asked if there had been any situation when the SatNavs had got them out of real trouble. Among the majority who gave a negative answer, several skippers stressed that thanks to their SatNavs they were never in real danger, as they always knew their precise position. Others pointed out that SatNav took a lot of the stress out of cruising, relieving the worries of a doubtful position. While agreeing on its usefulness, three skippers were wary of relying on it totally, either because it could break down in a critical situation or because many charts of less frequented areas still contain some errors, so that an uncharted reef can still be hit whether one has SatNav or not.

Tony Pearse of *Vahine Rii* gave an example of when, although not getting him out of real trouble, his SatNav had proved its worth. Having taken local people out night fishing near the Haapai group in Tonga, one of the Tongans on board was badly injured when a humpbacked whale was hooked by mistake. In spite of the darkness Tony was able to make his way to the nearest island with a hospital because he had kept his position accurately fixed all night with the help of his SatNav.

Among the three skippers who stated that SatNav had got them out of real trouble, two boats were nearly lost in the Tuamotus, aptly called by Captain Cook the 'Dangerous Archipelago'. In both cases SatNav helped the skippers assess correctly the strong current which otherwise might have put the boats on a reef during the night. Compared to the recent past, many more boats now cruise in the Tuamotus as a direct result of having SatNav on board. Jean-Marc Faubert, who has a SatNav himself on *Kouros*, shrewdly remarked, 'SatNav certainly gets you out of danger, but having it on board is what gets you into dangerous situations in the first place. Without SatNav most people simply would not dare go into places like the Tuamotus.'

The number of radars has also increased on cruising boats, eleven boats in the survey being equipped with radar. The six different makes gave a mixed performance and were rated an average 7. However, the majority of these skippers agreed on the usefulness of radar, eight skippers using their radar frequently, especially near landfall, while one of its devotees had even tracked squalls and waterspouts on his screen.

On the eight two masted boats, their radar scanner was mounted on the mizzen mast, while on two sloops the scanners were on or just above the spreaders. The smallest boat equipped with a radar was *Ave del Mar*, which had the scanner on a special mounting on the aft deck. The skipper Jamie Bryson, who had learnt to value his radar in his home waters of Alaska, found it just as useful among the reefs and low atolls of the South Pacific.

David Samuelson had no radar on his *Swan II*, but praised his Watchman radar detector, which was always switched on during night watches, to signal the presence of any boat in the vicinity using its radar.

Considering such an array of instruments I asked each skipper what he considered to be his most useful electronic instrument. By far the most votes (18) were cast in favour of the depth sounder, with SatNav coming in second place with 9 votes. To the opposite question of the most useless instrument, the answers were more varied, ten skippers putting RDF at the top of their useless list and nine VHF. These items were quoted as useless, not so much because of their performance, but as regards their relevance in ocean cruising.

What did come in for a lot of criticism because of poor performance and lack of reliability were electronic instruments for measuring such things as wind speed, wind direction, and the speedometer, all of which are of limited use when cruising offshore. Again and again skippers complained about the poor quality of electronic instruments, and that a higher price did not guarantee a better quality product than a cheaper make. A common complaint was that equipment built for a marine environment was sometimes not properly sealed and so the terminals corroded in a short time.

Corrosion is the prime problem with instrumentation afloat, especially if equipment is used only for short periods. Björn Boe Nielsen of *Palma*, an ex-merchant marine officer, kept his SatNav and VHF on all the time, advising others to do the same, as being the best way of keeping moisture out of electronics. Another suggestion was to seal the backs of the instruments properly before they were installed on the boat, thus minimising the dangers of a breakdown caused by corroded terminals.

When equipment did break down, it was often impossible to have it repaired locally, nor did the skippers in the survey have much success when the faulty equipment was sent back to the manufacturers. After-sales service appears to have deteriorated in recent years, especially once the user is thousands of miles away. As a result many skippers had given up on their faulty equipment and learnt to manage without it. Max Graveleau of *Hispania*, who had more experience than many with broken and working instruments, stressed, 'Reliability is the most important aspect of an instrument meant for ocean cruising. It is better for them to be simpler and have less functions, as long as they can be *relied* on to do the job they are supposed to do.'

RADIO

An increasing number of cruising boats carry radio transmitters on board and these fall into three broad categories, VHF radio-telephones, maritime transceivers, commonly known as SSB sets, and amateur radio transceivers, also known as ham radio.

The majority of boats (35) had a VHF set, although 20 skippers said that they used them very little. The commonest use of this radio was to call up ports on arrival. On the other hand, several boats kept their VHF on standby while at anchor and used them as a telephone to keep in touch with other boats nearby. The greatest variety of makes was found in this section, most of the 23 different brands performing well, reflected in the average rating of 8·6. The commonest make was Sailor, the five sets all receiving the maximum 10, as did the four Icoms. Two of the latter were handheld and were part of the crew's preparation for the eventuality of abandoning ship.

For this purpose emergency radio beacons (EPIRB) were carried by 24 boats. Amongst these, four were new, while fourteen had already been serviced and had new batteries put in. There is no way of assessing their performance, as they activate only when disaster strikes, so having them serviced regularly is almost the only way to check them.

For long distance communications an increasing number of sailors prefer to use amateur radio, which has been a popular hobby ever since the earliest days of radio, with countless enthusiasts throughout the world. By international agreement amateur operators can only transmit on certain frequencies, which are reserved for their use.

In the Pacific survey sixteen boats had an amateur radio set, although only eight used it frequently. There was a large variety of models in use, which performed well and were given an average rating of 8·8 by their owners. They also assessed the usefulness of having amateur radio, some regarding it as an important safety aid, while others enjoyed it as an excellent hobby to pursue while cruising. For the countries where regulations are less stringent, amateur radio is an excellent way of maintaining contact with family and friends. As Juan Ribas of *Abuelo III* said, 'I only use the radio to tranquillise my mother.'

The serious amateur operators had put a lot of thought into the type and positioning of their antennae, of which an optimum solution has yet to be found for sailing boats. This problem was reflected by the great variety of antennae in use, from straight wires to dipoles, whips, hustler heads or the classic use of the backstay as a random wire. Normally these antennae were used in conjunction with an antenna tuner.

The switch over to amateur radio was apparent in the small number of boats equipped with maritime SSB sets. Out of the four owners, only one used his set regularly and they all rated the usefulness of this equipment as very low. In fact it was pointed out by several operators that the latest amateur radio sets can also be used on the maritime frequencies by a simple modification. Although this modification is illegal in most countries, the people who carried it out stressed that they never transmitted, but used their modified sets mainly to pick up the more detailed international maritime weather reports.

There are now many amateur maritime networks in operation throughout the world, keeping track of boats on passage, supplying them with the latest weather information and providing a link with the outside world in case of emergency. The yachting grapevine has taken over the airwaves and an increasing number of cruising boats are now keeping in touch via the amateur wave bands. The Seven Seas Cruising Association, an international voyagers' club publishes an up to date list of the principal maritime networks. It can be obtained against a small fee from the SSCA, P.O. Box 2190 Covington, Louisiana 70434, USA.

Amateur radio is rapidly becoming the yachtsman's best friend at sea, while Al Huso of *Potpourri* went as far as describing an amateur set as the best safety measure to have on a boat. Unfortunately getting a licence for a mobile unit is still difficult in a number of countries. Several skippers felt that one should be allowed to carry an amateur set on board, provided it was only used in real emergencies, and that a basic licence should be accepted in such a case. Some smaller countries issue amateur radio licences for non-residents for a minimal fee, helping those who try to circumvent the cumbersome and outdated regulations in their own countries, but who wish nevertheless to preserve a semblance of legality.

The situation among the twelve circumnavigators accurately reflects the way things are moving in the radio world on cruising boats. Two boats had no radio equipment at all, nine boats had VHF radio telephones, although some of these were used very little. Two boats also had SSB transceivers, which were

Amateur radio has gained enormous popularity among cruising people. The advances in electronics have brought small compact equipment within the reach of most people's pockets. Dana Crumb on *Whistler* keeps regular contact with many cruising friends.

used even less, while on the other hand the five amateur radio operators used their equipment extensively. All five amateurs kept in contact with amateurs on other boats, while three of them also kept regular schedules with land based stations.

Steering

In the Pacific survey two thirds of the boats (32), including all the ten largest ones, had wheel steering, while 22 boats were steered by a tiller. These owners appeared more contented, giving their tillers an average rating of 9·4, compared to the 8·7 given to wheel steering. Four boats had both wheel and tiller, an arrangement highly recommended by their skippers. Of the boats with wheel steering, three skippers specifically stated that they would prefer tillers, and one of these was in fact making this change. Singlehander Ted Judd of *Grendel* rated his wheel 0 and was in the process of fitting a tiller and an outboard rudder, incorporating a trim tab for more efficient selfsteering.

Most of the wheel steerings (20) were of the cable type, with which their users appeared to be satisfied, giving this system an average rating of over 9.

A similar high rating was given to the four hydraulic systems. The rest of the boats, mostly the older ones, had diverse systems, which in spite of their age functioned well. The least satisfied skippers were the two who had rod steering, Juan Ribas of *Abuelo III* being particularly annoyed at the frequency with which the belts kept breaking, in one instance putting both the boat and the lives of the crew in danger.

SELFSTEERING AND AUTOPILOTS

A factor which has contributed more than anything else to the increase in the number of people undertaking long ocean voyages is undoubtedly the advent of reliable selfsteering gear. This has been paralleled in recent years by the development of automatic pilots for smaller craft, giving ocean voyagers an even wider choice in making their lives more comfortable.

Selfsteering was examined in all the major surveys, but in spite of the fact that all boats surveyed in Suva had sailed considerable distances offshore, it was surprising that six of them had neither selfsteering gear nor autopilots. Among the remaining 56 boats, 42 (68 per cent) had some kind of wind-vane selfsteering, while 27 boats (44 per cent) had an automatic pilot. Fourteen boats had both selfsteering and autopilot, hence the percentage discrepancy. Of the total number of selfsteering devices, 29 were commercially made and were rated higher (average rating 8) than the 13 homemade ones (rated 6·7), although the home built gears attracted higher marks when they had been copied from proven models. Generally the well tried and proven models were given higher ratings by their owners. The most commonly used gear (7) was the UK made Aries, which got an average rating of 9·86. Of the five trimarans surveyed, three had selfsteering and their skippers were satisfied with their perfomance, giving them an average rating of 8.

Assessing the merits of a particular type of selfsteering device is a very subjective matter, as so much depends not just on the gear itself, but also on the sailing and handling characteristics of the boat in question, as well as on the skipper's skill in getting his boat perfectly trimmed and balanced. Best results were achieved by those able to fit a trim tab to their main rudder. The gears that incorporated a servoblade fared much better than the independent devices, which often proved to be under-powered in the boisterous sailing conditions encountered on some long ocean passages.

Because selfsteering devices are such an essential feature on any long distance cruising boat, I later made them the subject of a separate survey. In a sample of 50 cruising boats, 36 had selfsteering gears, 9 of which were homemade, the remaining 27 being stock designs. As in the previous survey, the largest number of these gears (12) were made by Aries, with an additional two having Monitor gears, which is an American design, almost identical to Aries. The remaining 13 were divided among 10 different makes, so a comparison between the various makes was impractical. Hydrovane was another UK-made gear also praised by its two owners, one of whom was a singlehander who used the gear even to sail him out of port. The Swedish-made Sailomat also scored highly on all points of sailing, its only disadvantage being its very high price, whereas in the case of the cheaper French-made Plastimo, its owner wished the manufacturers had made it 25 per cent larger and stronger. Overall, the 36 gears had been used on average 16,200 miles per boat, two years being the average time they had been in use, as several boats had only fitted selfsteering gear *after* the start of their voyages.

Only three boats among the fifty in the Pacific survey had neither a selfsteering gear nor autopilot. The decision against these aids was taken by the skippers either because their boats held their course quite satisfactorily by trimming the sails, or because the skippers held the view that a hand on the helm meant a pair of eyes always in the cockpit. Forty boats had selfsteering gears, eighteen also having an autopilot, while a further seven boats had only autopilots and no wind vane steering.

The most common make among the forty selfsteering gears was again the Aries, the 14 skippers giving it an average of 8·4. There were ten other different makes in use, while nine gears had been built by their owners. The overall average rating for all the gears worked out at 8·6, showing that the owners were generally satisfied with their performance and reliability. A growing number of voyagers are preferring to install an autopilot as well, to be used when conditions do not favour the wind vane. Overall the 25 autopilots were given a lower average rating of 7·5, which was not so much in respect of their performance as their reliability. The most common complaint was that, although most models had to be mounted in an exposed position, the design was not waterproof and this led to corrosion and breakdown. Among the ten different makes of autopilot, those which were in an enclosed position or formed an integral part of the steering attracted higher ratings.

In the case of selfsteering gears, the structural strength of the equipment was an essential factor mentioned by several skippers, who also suggested to other voyagers to bear this important point in mind, especially those planning longer voyages.

In the Cruising survey, among the nineteen gears which relied on a servoblade to provide additional force, on eleven boats the lines were led from the vane to the tiller, while on the remaining eight boats the steering wheel was fitted with a special drum to take the selfsteering lines. The latter

The functional stern of 36 ft double-ended *Hero* offers not only protection to the Sailomat selfsteering gear, but also provides stowage for other equipment. Sailomat also produce an autopilot attachment which connects to the servorudder and considerably reduces the consumption of power.

arrangement was generally satisfactory, but in a few instances the skippers did mention that their boats appeared slower to respond, and for this reason, three skippers of boats with wheel steering had auxiliary tillers fitted to take the selfsteering lines. Wheel drums fitted to mechanically driven steering systems consistently gave better results than those fitted to hydraulic ones.

Because of the hard use the gears were submitted to, several of the stock designs had to be strengthened or slightly modified. Nearly half the gears broke at some point, although in most cases could be repaired immediately. Several skippers admitted that the breakages were probably the result of poor maintenance, which was not always the fault of the users. Some manufacturers ignore this aspect and give little or no advice regarding the proper care and maintenance of the gears.

Ground Tackle

As docking facilities outside of Europe and North America are extremely limited, the boats surveyed spent most of their time in port at anchor. Ground tackle was therefore another major point of discussion both in the Cruising and Pacific surveys. In the former the majority of boats (85 per cent) used chain only with their main anchor, while nine boats used chain and line. To qualify as 'chain only', the boat in question had to have at least 100 feet of chain on its main anchor, although I found that in most cases boats carried twice that amount and even more. For extended cruising, chain has several advantages over line, not least of which is its better durability.

In the Pacific survey, the skippers were asked to assess their main anchor and as in the Cruising survey, by far the most common type in use was the plough. Amid the general satisfaction with this anchor, a few skippers warned of poor imitations of the CQR, which did not perform as well as the original (see Table 5). The average weight of the plough anchor was 47 lb, the eleven boats over 40 ft using this type of anchor having an average anchor of 52 lb, while the 24 boats under 40 ft had anchors with an average weight of 45 lb. The majority of boats carried anchors well in excess of what is considered an adequate weight for their particular length. This was equally true for the other types of anchor, the five Danforths having an average weight of 65 lb for boats over 40 ft and 53 lb for boats under 40 ft. The remaining types averaged 42 lb for the Bruce and Brittany anchors and 72 lb for the Fisherman anchors. In fact ten skippers specifically mentioned that they carried an additional heavy anchor (average 75 lb weight) to be used in case of severe storms or hurricanes. The majority of boats carried at least three anchors and these did not include light, folding anchors.

TABLE 5. *Main anchors, Pacific survey.*

Anchor type	No.	Average weight (lb)	Average rating
CQR/Plough	35	47	9
Danforth	5	58	8·7
Brittany	4	49	8
Bruce	3	42	7·5
Fisherman	2	72	7·5
Northill	1	30	9

Anchoring securely is a prime concern of the long distance voyager.

This concern for heavier ground tackle was also reflected in the choice of chain, 39 boats having ⅜", one ½" and ten 5⁄16" diameter chain. Compared to the Suva survey there was a definite increase in the weight of ground tackle, both chain and anchor. In line with the same tendency, a higher proportion of skippers preferred to anchor with chain only, 92 per cent having at least 100 ft of chain on their main anchor. The forty boats carrying in excess of 100 ft of chain and anchoring always with chain only, had an average of 240 ft of chain in their forepeak, several boats having additional lengths of chain for their second and even third anchors.

This insistence on more than adequate ground tackle shows the importance that long distance voyagers attach to being securely anchored under all conditions. Apart from the amount of chain, most boats also carried various lengths of anchoring warps, the average for the 48 boats equipped with line in addition to their chain being 400 ft per boat. These varied in size from ½" to a hefty 2½", although the majority of skippers were content with warps ranging in diameter from 5⁄8" to 1".

To cope with this heavy ground tackle 43 boats were equipped with a windlass. Generally the 28 hand operated ones gave less satisfaction and were

Rigid dinghies continue to be more popular for cruising because they stand up better to rough treatment.

rated an average 6·5. Five skippers specified that their windlasses were too small and that they should have equipped themselves with a more powerful one to deal with heavy chain and deep anchorages. Another common complaint was about corrosion to the aluminium housing on some windlasses, which did not stand up to the marine environment and exposure on the foredeck, even if the mechanism itself gave no cause for complaint.

The fifteen electric windlasses fared on the whole better in this respect and were given an average rating of 8.4 by their owners, seven of whom gave the maximum 10. On both types of windlasses some skippers had troubles with non-calibrated chain which tended to slip on the gypsy.

Tenders and Outboard Engines

In the Suva survey, loyalties were evenly divided between rigid dinghies and inflatables when I asked the skippers to rate their dinghy from the point of view of an overall yacht tender. The 43 hard dinghies (wood, plywood, fibreglass or aluminium) received an average rating of 8·6 as opposed to the 7·8 given to the 40 inflatables. Several boats had more than one tender, many of the larger boats carrying both a hard dinghy and an inflatable. The smaller boats were often forced to choose a one-and-only inflatable for lack of space.

Tenders were reassessed in the Pacific survey, in which the 39 inflatables received an average rating of 7, compared to the 8·7 given to the 31 rigid dinghies. Twenty boats had two tenders, while 13 of the hard dinghies were equipped with masts and sails, even if rigged only occasionally. The higher rating given to the hard dinghies was mainly because they are easier to row and stand up much better to rough treatment such as landing on coral and rocky beaches. Skippers also pointed out that a hard dinghy was better for rowing out a second or stern anchor in windy conditions. Hard dinghies also hold an outboard engine more easily, although it was mentioned that, precisely because they are easier to row, it is possible to dispense with an outboard altogether. On the other hand hard dinghies have certain disadvantages, mainly that they take up more space, can be a hazard in very heavy weather, are not good for diving from and have the annoying tendency to bang against the boat or selfsteering gear, especially in tidal waters.

Carrying the tender on davits is considered dangerous on passage and only three of the larger boats had davits, the remaining hard dinghies being carried on the coachroof, or in a few cases on the foredeck. *Jeux à Deux* had an ingenious dinghy in two sections which folded into each other for stowage.

Compared to earlier surveys, more boats now have an outboard engine for their tenders, 40 boats in the Pacific survey having an outboard, three of them possessing two. Among the eight different makes, the highest average ratings were given to the nine Yamaha engines (9·1) and the six Suzukis (8·9). The other ratings were: Mariner 8·2, Johnson 8, Evinrude 7·6, Seagull 7·3, Volvo and Mercury 7 each. When asked if they considered an outboard engine to be *essential* on a cruising boat, 21 skippers, most of them on the smaller craft, replied in the negative. Among the 29 who regarded an outboard as an essential piece of equipment, two skippers pointed out that they had used their outboards to move their boats when the main engine was broken. Others stressed their usefulness when having to anchor far from the shore, or when wishing to explore reef areas or rivers. As most inflatables are notoriously bad for rowing, several owners of such dinghies considered their outboard engines essential while cruising.

Liferafts

A significantly large number of the boats surveyed in Suva were not equipped with an inflatable liferaft, only 40 out of the 62 skippers considering it worthwhile to invest in this relatively expensive piece of equipment, while in the Pacific survey a higher percentage, 36 out of 50, had liferafts. Liferafts have earned themselves a rather bad name among small boat voyagers in recent years, although considering the remarkable rescues effected over the years when shipwrecked crews had been saved after long periods of time spent in liferafts, I regard this reputation as unjustified. It was surprising to find so many crews sailing without liferafts across an ocean where yachts have been lost with sad regularity, so I looked in more detail at the alternative arrangements made for abandoning ship.

Both in the Suva and Pacific surveys several skippers stressed that they had absolutely no intention of abandoning their boats and considered their chances of rescue to be much higher if they somehow managed to keep the damaged hull afloat. Several of these skippers were owners of steel craft, all of whom had built their boats themselves and had extreme confidence in the strength of their hulls. Tony Pearse was certain that his *Vahine Rii* could withstand a collision at sea and if he was to lose his boat it would most likely be on a reef, from where rescue would not be made simpler by a liferaft. Among those who felt that their chances of survival were stronger if they stayed with their boat was Robert Lowe of *Windrace*. Instead of a liferaft he had purchased seven inflatable bags with a buoyancy of one ton each. These were permanently attached to a diving cylinder and could be inflated inside the boat in a matter of minutes, providing sufficient buoyancy to keep the hull afloat.

On several boats without a raft, alternative preparations had been made in case disaster struck and the boat had to be abandoned. In the Suva survey, ten skippers were planning to use their inflatable dinghies, seven being kept permanently inflated on deck, while the other three had been fitted with CO_2 bottles for rapid inflation. Six of those without liferafts intended to save themselves in their rigid dinghies, three of them having been fitted with mast and sail for this purpose, the gear being permanently kept inside the tender. Two other crews relied on their Hawaiian paddling canoes for their rescue, which were lashed on deck and could be easily launched.

Several of the skippers without liferafts in the Pacific survey also intended to use their tenders, which were stowed in such a way as to be easily launched in an emergency. There were also emergency provisions stored either in the dinghies or nearby, and freshwater containers at hand on deck for this eventuality. Also, on boats with liferafts, skippers had taken additional precautions for abandoning ship. On thirty-five boats survival packs were kept in an accessible place when on passage, usually inside the boat near the companionway. Many skippers also pointed out that they always had a few jerrycans of fresh water lashed on deck, but kept only three-quarters full, so that they would float if thrown overboard.

The contents of the survival packs varied enormously, from the bare minimum to a well thought-out selection of essential items needed for a prolonged period in a liferaft or dinghy. Most crews kept their personal documents and money prepared in an accessible place. Five boats had portable VHF sets, which formed part of the survival kit and, even if not packed in it, were kept ready by the companionway. The advantage of the portable radio set was stressed by one skipper who said that they are a much more effective way than flares of drawing the attention of a passing ship, as often distress flares had not been seen in daylight by officers on watch. Some packs also had an extra EPIRB to indicate the liferaft's position.

Apart from concentrated food, the survival packs also contained fish hooks, solar cells, water stills and in one case a mirror flashlight. A plastic sextant was included by one skipper who wanted to be able to know his position accurately, while in two cases survival suits were added to the contents, as well as a reflecting blanket to protect the wearer from exposure.

A lot of thought had also gone into the receptacle containing the survival kit. In some cases these were floating containers or small plastic drums with wide mouths. Some packs were kept in sailbags or sealed plastic bags. One skipper had tied a lifejacket around the waterproof bag. One ingenious skipper had also modified his inflatable dinghy so as to be able to use his sailboard sail on it in an emergency.

For the majority of cruising boats carrying an inflatable liferaft, I found their average size to be of six places, many skippers preferring to buy a raft with more places than the number of their crew. This makes sense considering the restricted space inside the liferaft and the length of time one might have to spend there before being rescued. In the Pacific survey, the average age of the liferafts was five years and the majority were serviced regularly, on average about every two and a half years. Liferafts can now be serviced in all major transit centres and cruising skippers take advantage of this fact when passing through places like Gibraltar, Canaries, Panama, Tahiti, Suva, New Zealand, Singapore or Durban. In a few instances the service on the liferafts had been carried out by the skippers themselves.

The majority of the liferafts were kept on deck, either mounted on the coach roof, aft or fore decks, while eleven were kept in a more protected place, either in the cockpit, in special lockers or even inside the boat. Because the raft containers are not always fully waterproof, an increasing number of people prefer to keep the liferafts in a protected, easily accessible place near the cockpit. This is certainly advisable considering the limited time one might have in which to abandon the boat if the hull was badly holed and sinking rapidly. It is for this reason that I am reluctant to dismiss the usefulness of an inflatable liferaft altogether. After all, small boat voyagers have always believed in the principle of wearing both belts and braces.

The Sweet Lemons of Honeymead

'No problem, we'll fix it,' exclaimed Chester with a cheerful smile after helping me dismantle my starter motor. 'But first, tell me what you've been up to since we last saw you in Fiji.'

As I started recounting our numerous adventures, which throughout the previous year had been punctuated by a series of engine failures and gear breakdowns, a smile crept across the face of this witchdoctor of engines. The last breakdown had occurred on the way to Rabaul in Papua New Guinea, as we were negotiating the straits between the islands of New Ireland and New Britain, notorious for strong currents. As the wind dropped completely, I attempted to start the engine, but in vain, the starter motor would not budge. In slow motion, the landmarks on the nearby coast started floating by in reverse order as *Aventura* was slowly taken backwards by the current. Fortunately, before too long a breeze sprang up and we managed to tack into Rabaul's landlocked harbour the next day to drop anchor next to *Honeymead*.

'You certainly have been plagued by a lot of problems, so now it's time we found their cause and put them right once and for all,' was Chester Lemon's comment. His approach to engines and anything to do with them had always been methodical, helped both by his training as a ship's engineer and the many years spent as a farmer, when he could rely on no one but himself to repair his farming equipment. On *Honeymead*, he had built a proper workshop which often acted as an operating theatre for bits of broken gear, although Chester's reputation as 'Mr Fixit' was earned not so much for the work carried out for the benefit of his fellow sailors, as for the help he gave to the people of the islands visited by *Honeymead*. Once Chester's mechanical wizardry became known, a string of broken outboard engines, water pumps or generators would be brought for him to resurrect and he was not a man to refuse to help.

The goodwill left behind by the Lemons was remarkable, as we discovered for ourselves as we sailed down the coast of New Guinea, one year after *Honeymead* had passed that way. We quickly learnt it was to our advantage to say we were friends of the Lemons, as in many a village this information was greeted with 'Ah, Chester and Norma, what wonderful people!', the crew of *Honeymead* being remembered with great affection.

Aventura and *Honeymead* first became intimately acquainted during a squall in Papeete harbour, when a poorly moored boat dragged its anchor down the line of boats, tripping several other anchors on its way. The struggle to keep *Aventura* and *Honeymead* from damaging each other or ending up on the rocks was our introduction to our neighbours, the successful outcome of which was our continuing friendship. From Tahiti, we met again in Tuvalu and Fiji, finally parting wakes as Chester and Norma headed for home to make the acquaintance of their grandchildren after a grand six-year tour of the Pacific.

After twenty years of dairy farming in Queensland, when their children had flown the parental nest, the Lemons decided to change their life style, sell everything and go cruising. Chester chose a Roberts 43 design for its spaciousness and ease of construction and in two years built and fitted out the fibreglass *Honeymead* himself. Then the farm was sold, they bade farewell to their children and set sail for distant horizons. Not for the Lemons a leisurely shakedown cruise, however, as they pointed *Honeymead*'s bow across the width of the Pacific, island hopping to Hawaii and then to Alaska. In waters where an Australian yacht is a rarity, the welcome they received from the people of Alaska, as well as the magnificent scenery, provided the highlight of their cruise. Sailing down the west coast to British Columbia and the United States gave Chester his first opportunity to visit his home country again after quarter of a century. He had left his native Oklahoma as a very young conscript in 1941 and spent the war with the US Navy in the Western Pacific. During a brief stopover in Brisbane for 'Rest and Recuperation' he met Norma, a young schoolteacher. Before the war was over, they were married and Chester decided to make Australia his new home.

In Rabaul, we visited together the multitude of relics left from the Japanese

Souvenirs of their lengthy voyaging decorate Chester and Norma's floating home.

wartime occupation of that harbour and Chester explained his interest in cruising through the Western Pacific.

'I spent the entire war cooped up in the engine rooms of various ships, never seeing any of the islands we sailed by: now I plan to go to all those places which I had missed seeing as a young man.'

The brief spell spent ashore visiting the family in Australia after six years of cruising had convinced both Chester and Norma that life afloat had much to offer and in Rabaul they were making plans to sail to Japan. No route appears to be too difficult for the Lemons and few boats have covered as interesting an itinerary as *Honeymead*.

With my starter motor repaired and many other mechanical problems straightened out by my skilled friend, our courses diverged in Papua New Guinea, *Aventura* setting sail westward for home and *Honeymead* continuing her trip down memory wake to the Philippines, Hong Kong and finally Japan. Having completed a circumnavigation of the Pacific, to do the same in the Indian Ocean appeared a logical sequence and one year later *Honeymead* was to be found leaving Singapore and the Malacca Straits behind, heading for Mauritius.

Honeymead's progress is regularly brought up to date by descriptive letters from Norma, who wields the pen just as skilfully as her skipper wields the spanner. However, during a short stopover in the island of Mayotte, north west of Madagascar, the skills had to be temporarily reversed.

'While in this beautiful corner of the world, I was suddenly confronted with serious doubts about half of us,' wrote Norma. 'Not long after we arrived, Chester suffered a gall bladder attack. He had to be flown back in a hurry to Reunion, where one gall bladder, twenty-three gallstones and an appendix were removed by the island's top surgeon. I stayed with poor *Honeymead* and, to show her displeasure at being deserted by her beloved captain, she started behaving badly. Every possible thing broke down, so that at one stage I had no toilet, no stove, no main engine, no generator and was faced with the prospect of no lights either as the batteries got flatter and flatter. Only the solar panels held things together and I surely appreciated their help. Finally, via the ham radio, I was able to send a lengthy message to Chester in hospital, listing all my problems. Back came very detailed instructions on how to fix *everything* and miraculously I, who am the world's very worst Mrs Fixit, soon had all problems solved. Desperation surely is a powerful driving force!'

Mr Fixit himself was soon returned to Norma with the surgeon's guarantee that he was good for another fifty years of sailing. That is obviously what they intend to do, because as soon as the skipper was back on board, *Honeymead* pointed her bows towards Kenya. After a lengthy stay there and in the Seychelles, the Lemons called for a second time at one of their favourite spots, the Chagos archipelago. Thailand and Malaysia were the next ports of call on *Honeymead*'s return journey to Australia.

Lately, an element of doubt appears to have crept into Norma's thoughts about cruising life.

'Suddenly I am dreaming of gallons of water gushing from a tap at the mere flick of a wrist, of a toilet that responds nobly to the push of a button, of night after night of uninterrupted sleep and of a sky that doesn't have to be continually watched for the first sign of rotten weather. . . . . Still, the last ten years have been marvellous, so when it comes to making the big decision, we may very well back down.'

Undecided what to do next, the Lemons are even toying with the idea of a circumnavigation, considering it disgraceful that they have never left the Pacific or Indian Oceans. Whatever they decide, they certainly show that age is no barrier to an active cruising life, nor to enjoying oneself to the full. The secret maybe is in their attitude, positive thinking being the driving force behind the sweet Lemons of *Honeymead*.

Duen's *Conversion for World Cruising*

Graceful and striking, all eyes turn towards her as *Duen* sails into an anchorage. Gaff-rigged, top masts, and jibs set flying, *Duen* is a ship run and rigged as a sailing boat from the last century. Behind the beauty lies a tale of hard work and a continuing heavy load of maintenance, for keeping up this kind of timber vessel requires a rare dedication. Not every antique boat has been lucky enough to find just such dedicated owners as Albert and Dottie Fletcher.

Duen was quite different, a scruffy fishing vessel of uncertain years, when the Fletchers first set eyes on her in 1971 in a small port in Norway. It was Albert's romantic imagination that looked past the disused fishing gear, derelict hydraulic piping, rust, grease and oil and could already picture in his mind's eye the promised beauty of *Duen*. The 50 ft hull was solid and had been well cared for and with her double ended traditional lines, adapted to the rough conditions of the North Sea, she promised to become a sea-kindly cruising boat. So they bought her.

If Dottie had inspected the engine room, the story might have been different, for *Duen* was powered by an ancient Rapp one cylinder semi-diesel engine with a one ton flywheel, promptly nicknamed Rapp the Monster. It had to be started with a compressed air bottle and every hour on the hour seventeen holes had to be oiled, twelve grease cups turned and five wicks filled, a not very pleasant task at sea in the dark, smelly, hot engine room.

For eighteen months in Norway, the Fletchers worked solidly, 12 to 18

Many years of hard work have transformed *Duen* from a shabby fishing vessel to a stylish sailing craft.

hours a day, gutting her, tearing out the old equipment and turning her slowly into the cruising boat they had dreamed of. The strength of the 50 ft hull, with a beam of 18 ft and a draft of 8 ft was impressive. The 9 by 9 inch frames were only seven inches apart, the two inch pitch pine outer hull being held together by four double sets of stringers fastened entirely by trunnels. In the cold winter they worked on the interior and in the warmer weather on the spars and rigging. They kept the Norwegian style pilot house and first set sail with *Duen* as a gaff rigged ketch with two short masts. Sailing alone and not being very experienced sailors, they were glad of the short rig. They learned as they went along, coast hopping southwards from Norway in search of warmer weather.

After a pleasant time in the Mediterranean and now more confident in their navigation and seamanship, they prepared to cross the Atlantic and take *Duen* back home to California. In the Caribbean however they lost the desire to rush; cruising had become a way of life and *Duen* their home. Joined by some of their family, they successfully chartered and spent several years in the Caribbean.

Albert then carried out the first of *Duen*'s transformations. Rapp the Monster was replaced and the pilot house dismantled, as it provided too much windage. With more space on deck, Albert could lengthen the boom and gaff and he also increased the sail area with a topmast. All the new spars he adzed out himself on the beach at Bequia.

When they finally got to California, Albert set about the third and final conversion for *Duen*. Now he had the experience and knowledge, he knew exactly what to do to turn her into a fine sailing vessel. In nearly a year of hard work Albert designed and made all the new spars, metal work and rigging. Then the Fletcher's set out across the Pacific in *Duen* as she is now, her varnished hull gleaming, a ketch with taller rig and jibs flying to the long bowsprit.

As might be expected for the owners of such a distinctive vessel, the Fletchers are not without character either. Albert is a burly Californian with a bushy black beard, tattooed arms and describes himself as a compulsive tool collector. Dottie, with her twinkling eyes, seems always to be laughing and I was quite surprised to find out that the young lad coiling ropes on deck was not her son but her grandson. *Duen* has often cruised for long periods with three generations on board and keeping the happy atmosphere on board ship owes much to Dottie's sense of humour.

Maintaining *Duen* is a time-consuming and costly business, the boat swallowing up far more money than Albert and Dottie ever spend on themselves. If they cannot afford to keep her going, Albert would prefer to sell *Duen*, than to let her deteriorate. To help with the maintenance bills, the Fletchers take on paying crew and charter when they can. When I last saw them in Australia, they were delighted to be doing a television film sailing up the Great Barrier Reef. Everything helps to keep *Duen* going, although knowing Albert's talents and capacity for hard work, I am sure that *Duen* is in no danger of ever being neglected and she will continue to grace the oceans as a reminder of the past glory of sail.

CHAPTER THREE

Living Afloat – the Practical and Administrative Aspects

Once a boat is chosen and equipped for a cruise and the conveniences of one's homeport left behind, problems of an entirely new nature start to loom over the horizon. Whether experienced or green, whether cruising on a shoestring or in great style, all long distance voyagers have to deal with certain practical matters such as the transfer of money overseas, forwarding mail, ordering spares and charts, and a host of other problems. These aspects are seldom mentioned when the beauty of blue water cruising is spoken of, yet their importance cannot be underestimated, for the success of many a cruise can be undermined by such apparently simple things that the skipper had failed to prepare for.

The Cruising Survey

Over a period of one year cruising in the Pacific from New Zealand to Tonga, Kiribati and Fiji, I interviewed every cruising boat I came across, trying to find out from their crews how they cope with these problems. As many of them were also sailors of considerable experience, I also asked them to make some practical suggestions to would-be voyagers. The 'Living Afloat' section of the survey ran to sixty questions concerning all practical matters of day to day cruising.

I started my work in New Zealand, where many boats which I had met previously in various corners of the Pacific were avoiding the cyclone season by passing the summer in the serene beauty of North Island's ports and coves. I had already interviewed some of the crews for my previous survey and I spent many a pleasant evening discussing these matters with my cruising colleagues, all of whom seemed to be as interested as myself in finding the best solutions to these practical problems.

In order to be sure of obtaining meaningful results, the boats surveyed had to fulfil two criteria. First, to have sailed a minimum of 5,000 miles away from base; and second, to have been cruising continuously for at least one year. As my data-gathering progressed I could afford to become more selective, trying

Papeete waterfront, port of call for most long distance voyagers.

whenever possible to talk to some of the long term voyagers, for whom cruising really is a way of life. The 50 boats included in the survey had covered a total of 1,190,000 miles on their present cruises, i.e. an average of 23,800 miles per boat, which is more than the circumference of the earth. In fact, the mileage would have been much higher if I had included in my calculation the total number of miles covered by the boat or skipper in question. Several of these had sailed many more miles in their long sailing careers, such as the Hiscocks on the various *Wanderers*, the Giesekings on *Lou I, II*, and *III*, the Calmés on *Karak* and many others. *Merry Maiden* and *Diogenes* were on their second circumnavigation, while *Fortuna* and *Gambol* had both just completed their circumnavigations in Fiji. There were also two recent Cape Horners in this select lot, *Shangri-La*, claiming to be the first catamaran to make an east to west passage, and *Tehani III*. Jan Swerts, the Belgian singlehander of *Tehani III*, was unfortunately the only skipper I could not interview in his own boat as he had recently lost her on a reef in Fiji's treacherous Eastern Group.

For all the variety of boats and people encountered, the typical cruising boat turned out to be surprisingly similar to the findings of the survey I carried out the year before in Suva, 38 ft long with an average crew of 2·4. Sailing approximately 6,000 miles per year, the average time spent on the

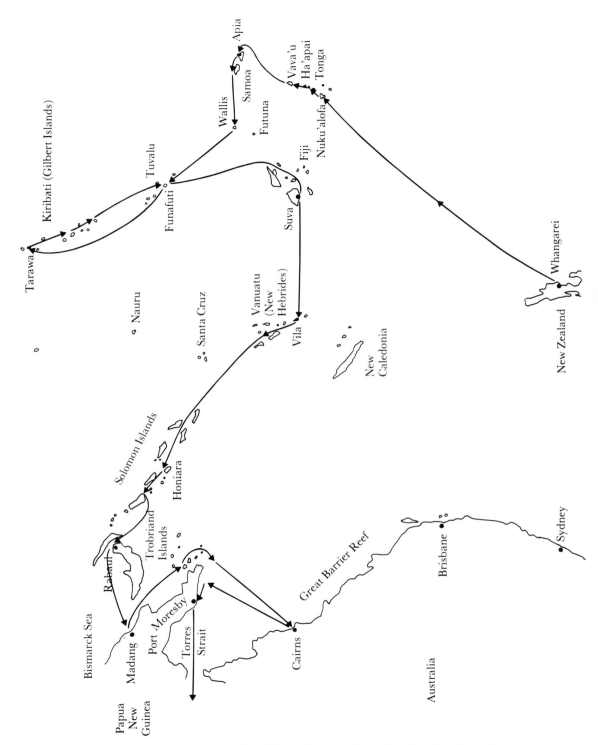

MAP C *Aventura*'s track while collecting data for the Cruising Survey

Willy and Marion Zech are cruising in style on their *Spirit of Cockpit.*

present cruise was four years. Out of the total of 50, 38 boats were crewed by a couple, either alone, or in eight cases accompanied by their children.

Many findings of the Cruising survey were confirmed by the Pacific survey, while others were more thoroughly investigated. One of the main conclusions five years after the first survey was that the profile of the long distance ocean voyagers had certainly changed over the years, with 43 of the crews featuring in the Pacific survey consisting of only two people, nearly all of them couples, whether married or not. Six of these couples had one child, and seven of them two children sailing with them. Only three boats had a crew of three and in two of these cases this third crew member was also a grown up member of the family. There was only one singlehander and three skippers who sometimes singlehanded and at other times took variable numbers of crew, usually one other person. On over forty boats there was a woman permanently on board, while with fourteen crews taking their children to sea, ocean cruising appears to have become very much a family affair.

Finances

The financial aspect of world cruising is undoubtedly one of the most important factors to be considered before setting off. Unfortunately in today's age of permanent inflation, finances continue to be the single problem causing most concern to the majority of voyagers and the lack of finance a major reason for halting a cruise. In all the surveys I was gratified that out of the total of well over one hundred crews interviewed on financial matters, only two declined to give me exact figures, one claiming that he had never even attempted to work out the approximate cost of cruising. All the rest gave me precise details on their budgeting, expenditure, source of income, transfer of funds etc., and as this data was gathered over a period of five years, it allowed me to make a statistical analysis based on these figures. As the US dollar is the most widely used international currency, I converted all costs quoted in other currencies into dollars.

CRUISING EXPENDITURE

To the crucial question of how much people spent during one year of cruising, I received a wide range of figures from $2,000 to $22,000 per boat per year, both of these boats having a crew of two. Such extremes however were rare, most of the figures quoted by the other crews being significantly grouped around the mean. To allow for the different numbers of crew, I calculated the average cost per crew member, counting children under the age of ten as half, and those over ten as whole. This resulted in an average annual cost of cruising of $2,947 per person. By a different method of calculation, that of finding the mean cost per person per boat first and then averaging these results, I arrived at a figure of $3,406 per person per year. The figures quoted by each crew included all living expenses, maintenance and repair costs, even the buying of souvenirs, but did not include insurance premiums, which could be as high as $2,000 per year for boats cruising in areas considered as high risk by the insurance companies.

Two years later, when I carried out a survey among a dozen circumnavigators, these figures were confirmed by the new findings. Although the total cost of a world voyage varied widely, from a minimum of $8,000 to a maximum of $43,000, both voyages lasting three years, the average cost per circumnavigation worked out at $24,500. As the average length of these voyages was three years and nine months, the cost per boat per year amounted to $6,500. With an average crew of two, this figure comes very near to the one quoted above, of approximately $3,000 per person per year.

In the Pacific survey, I was also quoted a wide range of figures for the cost per year, although the average worked out at $8,490 per boat. As the size of crew varied slightly from boat to boat, I calculated an average figure per person per year, again counting children under ten as half and older children as adults. This resulted in an average annual cost of $3,600 per person, a reasonable increase on earlier figures allowing for continually rising prices.

Although the above figures are only intended as a guideline, I would like to make some points for the benefit of those who take budgeting seriously. There are a few spots which can quickly drain the resources of the unwary, such as Tahiti, and these are places which should be treated with care by those on a tight budget. Another factor to be kept in mind when planning a budget is the continual rise in the price of fuel. Also, as some of the developing countries are experiencing problems with their exports and are often short of foreign currency, fuel is becoming difficult to obtain in a few places, and is occasionally unavailable for outsiders. Another item which can add considerably to expenditure is the cost of inland travel in the places visited.

BUDGETING

The material values and obsession with money that characterise western society were often among the main reasons why some of the sailors I met on my way around the world had left for a life at sea. This was perhaps the reason why more than half of those interviewed (28) in the Cruising survey did not operate a budget at all, just keeping an eye on expenditure in a vague way. Nevertheless practically all skippers, or more often their wives, were able to quote me the exact cost of their voyages. Georges Calmé of *Karak* reiterated the traditional principle of French good housekeeping when he said that, 'We try and live below our income like we have always done, which means that we try and economise all the time and in this way make ends meet.'

The people who kept a proper budget were generally those who were relying on a fixed monthly income, whether from pensions, investments or savings. Fourteen boats operated a monthly budget, which had to cover all expenditure. An additional two boats had a fixed budget for food alone and I found that only six boats had an itemised annual budget with allowances for living expenses, boat maintenance, insurance premiums, etc. The fourteen boats who operated a monthly budget kept this at an average of $512.50 per month, that is $6,150 per year. As all these boats who ran a monthly budget had an average crew of two the cost per person came out very close to the average figure indicated earlier.

On the subject of boat maintenance, only five skippers kept a separate budget for this purpose alone. The average allowance for repairs and maintenance varied from 25 per cent to 50 per cent of the general budget expenditure and in several instances I was told that a capital replacement, such as a new dinghy or sails, also had to come out of this allowance. Several skippers who did not operate a special maintenance budget complained that the upkeep of their boats swallowed up more than half of their annual cost of cruising. This was particularly true in the case of several older wooden boats, which demanded continuous attention, but some of the largest boats in the survey, made of other materials than wood, were equally hard and costly to maintain.

Several owners told me that they aimed to keep their boat in tip top condition as a way of protecting their capital investment. Albert Fletcher of *Duen* fought a continuous battle to keep his traditional Norwegian fishing vessel in the best state possible, but he did not seem daunted by the mammoth task.

'It's the boat that eats the money, our personal needs don't compare with what the boat swallows. As long as we can keep up the boat we will hold on to it, otherwise we'd rather sell it. Many boats are neglected after the first euphoria is over. I've seen it happen countless times. We protect our investment and our lives by keeping the boat in the best condition. A boat should always be in a seaworthy condition.'

SOURCES OF INCOME

As the ages differed as widely as the financial resouces of the crew, I subdivided them into age groups, which enabled me not only to investigate costing more closely, but also to analyse their source of income. In some cases where the crew fell into different age groups, I included the boat under the age of the skipper, especially as in some cases the ladies opted for a lower age bracket, if they were near the borderline! As might be expected, it was the youngest age group which spent the least amount of money. The six crews which managed to cope with less than 1,400 dollars per person per year, admitted that they often had a lean time. This was also the only group to include boats which had left home with virtually no savings at all. In some places en route, where jobs were available, these crews were forced to stop and work in order to fund the continuation of their voyage.

Looking at the table, it would appear that the most prosperous group was the one in the 40–50 age bracket, but as this group also included some of the crews with larger boats, who specifically mentioned much higher maintenance and fuel bills, the average figures tend to give the wrong impression. In practice, I found that in real terms the crews with more money to spare were

TABLE 6. *Results of source of income questionnaire, Cruising Survey.*

Age	No. of boats	Average cost per person per year	Source of Income				
			savings only	savings & occasional work	pension &/or investment	no savings must work en route	charter
under 30	6	$1,383		2		3	1
30–40	24	$3,344	16	7	1		
40–50	8	$4,654	3	5			
50–60	9	$3,406	6		3		
over 60	3	$4,062		1	2		
Total	50		25	15	6	3	1

in the 30–40 age group, who generally had kept the size of their boats in tune with their age, that is between 30–40 feet, being thus able to spend their money on other things than maintenance and fuel bills.

Herb Payson, the witty skipper of *Sea Foam*, summed up many people's feelings when he said, 'The biggest inhibition to cruising is not having enough money, then letting things go . . . It takes all the pleasure away, the lack of money, the shortage of funds to have repairs carried out by specialists when necessary. The voyage should not be undercapitalised.'

Herb's wife Nancy, who had been listening quietly to our conversation, added her own piece of advice for intending voyagers, 'Nevertheless, better do it on a shoestring than not at all.'

From what I was told, it appeared that more than half the crews financed their voyages entirely from savings. Several crews did occasional work to replenish their funds in order to either extend their cruise or provide additional comforts. One of the skippers was financing his round the world cruise entirely by chartering and I found that at least five other boats relied heavily on taking paying crew or guests. It may be an easy way of funding the continuation of a voyage, but the number of disgruntled and frustrated skippers who complained about their fare-paying crew members shows that what is easiest is not always the most pleasant.

What other possibilities of earning money underway are there? Generally, these fell into two categories, work ashore and work afloat. In spite of the restrictions imposed by most countries, hardly anyone who was willing to work failed to find some kind of employment, although often they had to look hard and be content with working illegally in unskilled jobs.

Stuart Clay of *Gambol*, who has worked his way around the world, earning money as he went along, had the following advice to give to others in a similar situation. 'Try and have some kind of income so as not to have to rely on work all the time, because often it is not easy to find. Also have some savings to fall back on if no work is available.' Nevertheless Stuart did manage to replenish the kitty throughout his six year long circumnavigation, perhaps because he was always ready to accept any kind of work that came his way.

In a better position were the people who had skills enabling them to find work on other boats, either on local craft or on other cruising boats, such as boatbuilding, sailmaking, carpentry, mechanical or electrical engineering. There were also a few who took their work with them wherever they went, freelance writers, jewellery makers and even a stock market speculator, who tried to keep in touch with his stockbroker by telephone whenever he could. The medical profession was well represented among those interviewed and included several doctors and nurses. In a few places some of these were able to find temporary locum appointments, usually while local staff took their vacations. Ruth Abney, *Incognito*'s mate, is a qualified sailmaker and never seemed short of work. She was often seen stitching away at someone's damaged sail on the spacious floor of the Suva Yacht Club. 'If you have no regular income or savings, try and have a way of earning money as you go along,' she suggested.

A quite unusual and unexpected way of earning money cropped up during my stay in French Polynesia. Along with several other crews, I happened to be in Bora Bora exactly when the Italian film producer Dino de Laurentiis was desperately looking for extras for a new version of 'Hurricane', which was being filmed on what James Michener has described as the 'most beautiful island in the world'. As we all had to play the parts of American sailors in the 1920s, beards, moustaches and locks of hair fell under the ruthless shears of an Italian barber, but at least this sacrifice on the altar of art kept us all in beer for a long time to come. More work as film extras was forthcoming the following year on another film.

Earning money as a film extra is unfortunately a rare stroke of luck for the shortfunded world cruiser, but there are other ways of earning money en route. Sometimes it was not necessarily money that was earned, but the goodwill of local people, whether one managed to repair a faulty radio, a broken pump or outboard motor, or to stitch up a thumb split in two, as happened to Jean-Francois Delvaux, a radiologist from Paris, while cruising in Indonesia. Because cash still has limited usefulness in many of these remote places, it is just as well that the local goodwill is often translated into gifts of fruit, vegetables or even meat. Those who expect to run a tight budget during their world cruise should make sure that they have at least a good set of tools on board, so as to be able to do a job ashore if the occasion arises. Obviously those having specialised skills would be well advised to take the tools of their trade along with them.

CREDIT AND CASH TRANSFERS

One does not have to be a financial wizard to cope with money transfers, currency regulations and rates of exchange, and most people quickly learn to deal with all these things, when they are continuously changing the colour of their money. A few skippers told me that they carry all their funds in cash, either because they preferred this or usually because they came from countries with strict currency regulations and could not have money easily transferred overseas. The majority of boats carried little ready cash and arranged for their funds to be transferred to a local bank along their route either by cable or airmail transfer. A practice highly recommended by several skippers on arrival in a port was to ask the largest of the local banks to telex their bank back home requesting the transfer of funds. This rarely took longer than 48 hours, and the transfer charges cost about ten dollars.

Among those interviewed, only two skippers relied on the now rather outdated system of letters of credit, which they found to be a satisfactory but expensive arrangement. Another skipper received his pension by international money order, which he found slow and unreliable. Fourteen crews kept their funds in travellers cheques of one of the major currencies, recommending these as they cost only 1 per cent of the total value to buy, but generally yielded between 3 and 5 per cent more on exchange than ordinary banknotes. An added advantage is that travellers cheques are replaced by the issuing bank if lost or stolen.

Currency regulations vary enormously from country to country. In some places when money arrives at the bank from overseas, this can be issued in travellers cheques of a major currency. In more restrictive countries the incoming funds may have to be converted into the local currency, which may not be freely converted when one leaves. In such places it is wise to only transfer sufficient funds to cover immediate needs.

It was also recommended that a certain amount of loose cash be carried, preferably US dollars in notes of smaller denominations. The mystic attraction of the 'greenback' is still going strong throughout the world, some shopkeepers will give a better price on goods for them, while in some remote places travellers cheques cannot be cashed at all, and out of banking hours there is usually a barman or shopkeeper to be found who will change some dollars into local currency.

In today's world of instant credit, it was not surprising to hear from several well travelled skippers that they had now changed over to drawing their funds by using their credit cards. American Express operates a world wide scheme, which enables the card holder to draw up to $1,000 in travellers cheques on demand against a personal cheque. No extra charge is made for this service, which is now available in many locations around the world. In smaller countries, the American Express representative is usually only found in the capital. A booklet listing all addresses is available free from American Express. An increasing number of people also use Visa/Carte Bleue to obtain cash and the number of local banks offering this facility is spreading rapidly, although in most developing countries they are usually only found in the capital.

For those planning a long voyage it would be wise to obtain the various credit cards while still in permanent employment, as banks or credit companies may refuse to issue them later on, having little trust in the credit worthiness of sailors.

Similarly, for those intending to spend any length of time in Europe, it is advisable to open a checking or current account with one of the larger European banks, which automatically gives the account holder the possibility to draw limited amounts of cash at any bank displaying the Eurocheque sign. These can now be found not only in the remotest places in Europe, but also in North Africa and the Middle East, and even some banks in the Caribbean would cash a personal cheque accompanied by a Eurocheque card.

One of the irksome financial problems faced by world voyagers is the bond demanded by the authorities in French Polynesia. Every crew member, including children, who intends to spend more than a few days there must either be in possession of a valid return airline ticket to the country of origin, or deposit the equivalent sum in a bank in Papeete. Letters of credit are not accepted, nor is there any interest paid on the deposit, in fact an additional charge is made by the bank for holding the money. The bond can either be paid in over the counter in cash or travellers cheques or can be transferred by telex to the Banque Indo-Suez in Papeete by the applicant's personal bank. The money is returned before departure when commencing clearing out procedures. Visas of shorter duration can be obtained on arrival in most outlying islands, but for those planning to spend several months in French Polynesia the bond is virtually unavoidable. Obtaining a visa before arrival does not exempt one, as this visa cannot be extended beyond 30 days unless the bond has been deposited.

SHARING COSTS

Another topic of discussion with the skippers was the financial arrangements they made with friends or crews joining their boats. Twenty boats had never had friends join them for any length of time, while twenty others expected their guests who joined them to share in all costs. Some skippers even specified that they would expect their cruising friends to foot the whole bill for drinks. The remaining ten boats made little difference between friends and paying crew, charging them a flat rate ranging from three to ten dollars per day. The skippers who applied the flat rate principle to their guests found that this caused less disagreement than the sharing of expenses.

Of the total number of boats surveyed, twenty-eight never took on crew, being entirely self sufficient in this respect. As for those who took on crew, gone are the days when a deckhand could work his or her passage in return for his or her keep. All crews were expected to contribute towards costs to a larger or smaller degree. Eight boats generally took on crew only for longer passages and worked a shared expenses system. In these cases the crew were expected to help with the handling of the boat, cooking, washing up and taking watches. The skippers who preferred to charge a flat rate per day told me that they did not necessarily expect their crew to work, especially on the boats which charged a higher amount. On the other hand, one skipper who occasionally chartered his boat, while also having paying crew, always gave a share of the profit to these paying crew.

There was never any disagreement about the sharing of expenses on *Tarrawarra*. The crew, Steve, Tony, and Kim had been sailing together since they were teenagers.

Planning Ahead

MAINTENANCE SCHEDULES

Continuous cruising requires quite a bit of planning, yet I found that out of the 50 skippers in the Cruising survey, only 21 planned to stop after a certain number of months to carry out basic maintenance work, hauling and antifouling. Fourteen skippers told me that they planned on stopping every twelve months, one boat every nine months, and six boats every six months. The remaining 29 boats carry out all necessary work as they go along, stopping only when convenient or absolutely necessary. Susan Hiscock complained about the tedious chore of maintaining their 50 ft steel *Wanderer IV*, which is probably one of the reasons why they gave her up in favour of *Wanderer V*:

'We plan our voyage around weather systems, not around maintenance requirements. Still, we seem to spend one third of our time on maintenance, one third on writing and only one third on going ashore.'

Often, hauling out for antifouling had to be planned around where a slipway was available, or at least a grid and a good tidal range. For larger boats with more than 6 ft draft, it was sometimes difficult to find a suitable place to haul. The majority of boats were only hauled out once a year or even less often than that, and because of this many skippers preferred to use a hard vinyl antifouling paint, which enabled them to scrub the bottom underwater as soon as the first slime or growth started forming.

In my previous survey in Suva, I had found that the average time since the last application of antifouling worked out at eleven months per boat, although hardly any brand of antifouling appeared to give satifactory results after the initial six months under tropical conditions. Surprisingly enough the highest ratings were rarely given to the well known expensive brands, but often to copper rich paints, such as the ones used by the Navy. In two instances I was told of the excellent results achieved by using the special paint designed for submarines, but unfortunately this is not generally available. Good results were also reported with cheaper paints bought in tropical countries such as Venezuela, Costa Rica and Fiji and used by the local fishing boats. In the tropics where the danger from teredo worm is worst, boats with wooden hulls are most vulnerable, and more attention to both antifouling used, and the frequency it is applied, pays off.

SPARES AND REPAIRS

As well as the high cost in money and time of keeping a cruising boat in good running condition, most skippers emphasised the difficulty of obtaining even the simplest spares in some places. Because of this, many boats carried on board all essential spares. One skipper suggested that if this was not possible, at least have specification lists available to facilitate the ordering of spares. Dud Dewey, who had spent several years in restoring the schooner *Hawk* to her former beauty, knew what he was talking about when he gave the following piece of advice:

'Take every spare you feel you will need later on, as cruising with the problem of finding spares can be a nuisance, a trial. I carry twenty pounds of stainless steel nuts and bolts on my boat and I am continually supplying other boats who cannot find even such basic things in the South Pacific.'

Finding the skilled man to carry out specialist repairs can often be even more difficult than finding the necessary spare. Many skippers complained about unsatisfactory work carried out in some countries. Very often it became a matter of either getting on with the repair oneself or being stuck in some remote corner forever.

Nick Zeldenrust, of *Kemana*, an ex-officer in the Dutch Merchant Navy, who later emigrated to Canada, where he worked as a land surveyor in the middle of the North American continent, declared himself totally committed to the principle of self-help:

'Most of the worries on a boat are caused by maintenance. Before setting off, one should learn about electrical work, even take a course in diesel mechanics, which can be done by correspondence. You don't have to be all that good with your hands to be able to carry out simple repairs on your boat.'

The twelve circumnavigators whom I interviewed later encountered very few serious problems during their voyages, although by far the commonest breakdown was engine failure, which always seemed to occur in remote places where spares and repair facilities were difficult to come by. Ironically, these boats used their engines very little and according to their skippers, sailed an average of 95 per cent of the time. Maybe their engines failed just because they were used so infrequently. The other common failure was that of standing rigging, although all faulty rigging was discovered and repaired during routine checks in port. As well as essential engine parts, spare rigging wire and accessories seem high on the list of items to be carried by any boat sailing further afield.

While discussing the subject of repairs with skippers, I also asked them if they could carry out underwater work on their boats. Those who were in doubt about what was expected of them, I asked the specific question if they could, for instance, remove a line fouled around their propeller. In the case of every boat, I was assured that there was a mask and snorkel available and also that there was somebody who could dive overboard in an emergency. In the few instances where the skipper could not dive himself, either the mate or another crew member could do it, if such an action became necessary. In fact, thirteen boats carried full air tanks on board, which were rarely used for diving, but were kept for such an emergency. Two boats carried Hookah compressors, which enabled the crew to either work underwater, rescue a fouled anchor or more usually keep the hull free from growth.

Insurance

The possibility of a major or minor catastrophe must be at the back of every seafarer's mind, whether it is falling seriously ill in a foreign port, losing a mast or even the boat itself. Due to the high cost of insurance premiums for world cruising, I found that out of one hundred boats only 20 were fully insured, three were insured for a total loss only, while eight others carried insurance for third party claims only. Seven of the insured boats also carried insurance for gear and personal effects. Several of the boats had been insured previously in their home cruising areas, but the quotations rose so steeply for further afield (from $2–5,000 per year) that they had no choice except to cancel. *Ondine*, which was insured as far as Panama, having sailed extensively in Africa and South America, found its premium doubled and so the skipper kept only the third party insurance, while *Con Tina*, after being insured for four years in the Pacific, had so many troubles getting re-insurance, that the skipper cancelled the policy, went out and bought a heavy anchor. Several people regarded their large and heavy ground tackle, or their instruments, such as SatNav or radar, as their insurance policies.

Of the total number of boats less than a quarter had taken out medical insurance for all crew members, whereas in the case of life insurance, fifteen men had their lives insured but only five women. This did not necessarily mean that the skippers regarded their lives to be more valuable than those of their wives, but simply because many men had taken out life insurance while still working ashore and had kept these going when they left home.

Even if not insured, most boats had at least an allowance available for major repairs, replacement of vital equipment or medical expenses. Generally I was told that this allowance would come out of savings, although in ten cases a special fund has been set aside to cover just such an emergency. One skipper, who would not even consider insuring his boat, claiming that it would give him a false sense of security, had put aside enough money to buy another boat if he lost the present one. Two couples on two different boats carried with them valid undated air tickets, which would enable them to fly home in a medical emergency. At the other end of the resource scale, twelve boats did not have any reserve at all, only two of these being insured. For most of these crews even a minor mishap could put their cruise in jeopardy. It is one of the many calculated risks they take.

Mail

The receiving and forwarding of mail seems to cause more headaches to world voyagers than anything else. The stories of mail missed, lost, sent back or miraculously retrieved after several changes of address, never fail to crop up whenever cruising folk get together. General Delivery/Poste Restante continues to be the most widely used receiving address, although far from the most satisfactory. Asked to rate this service from one to ten, the skippers gave General Delivery an average rating of 7·6. A few people pointed out however that in the case of parcels or packets, the rating should have been much lower. Particularly poorly rated were the Post Offices in some Central American countries and in French Polynesia, where mail is only held for two weeks before being returned to sender. The next commonly used address was that of yacht clubs, which received a similar average rating of 7·6, some clubs being better than others in holding or even forwarding mail. Fourteen boats have also used Port Captains or Harbour Masters as a forwarding address and these were rated higher than clubs at an average 8·8, being particularly recommended in countries where post offices were not reliable (Bali), or would not hold General Delivery/Poste Restante mail (Mexico, Tahiti). Some of the boats also used embassies or banks to receive mail, although it was advisable to write first and ask for permission to use this service. The average rating given to banks and embassies for holding mail was 9, while American Express offices received a rating of 10 from the crews, who used its mail holding service for cardholders. In all cases it was recommended that 'Hold for Arrival' and the name of the boat should appear in bold letters on the envelope. One can always find out via the cruising grapevine the addresses of the best places for receiving mail that lie ahead. This is proving to be yet another advantage of amateur radio, as messages can be passed on quickly and effortlessly to other boats and missed mail can be immediately dispatched to the next port of call. Several German skippers strongly recommended the Trans-Ocean Club (Altenw. Heideweg 15, 2190 Cuxhaven 13, West Germany), which has a list of holding addresses for mail in many countries. A similar service offering contact addresses around the world is also offered both to full and associate members by the Seven Seas Cruising Association (PO Box 2190 Covington, Louisiana 70434, USA).

Loyal friend of the cruising fraternity, the postmistress of Opua Margaret Cavers always makes sure mail reaches its destination.

Charts

Navigation charts are very hard to obtain outside major ports and because of this the majority of the boats had made some provision to overcome this difficulty. Among the 50 boats in the Cruising survey, 17 left home with more or less all the charts needed for their intended voyage, while six skippers preferred to place orders with a chart agent in their own country as they went along. Just over half the boats (26) left home with some charts, usually for about half the voyage, relying afterwards on swapping or buying charts from other boats.

Some boats, though, leave home with even less than the bare minimum as Beverly Wilmoth told me smilingly over a cup of coffee on board *Aslan*:

'We left San Diego with only one chart on board, showing Hawaii as a tiny speck in the bottom corner. I sure don't know how we ever found it.'

Not only did they find Hawaii, but by the time I started work on this book, *Aslan* had already circled the globe and was back home in Texas.

A few skippers made a point of asking the officers of freighters for their used charts, which were usually given away and often included the latest corrections. Generally when charts changed hands between boats, the going rate was slightly less than half of the official price. A few boats also kept a good supply of tracing paper on board to copy borrowed charts, or at least the section of interest to them. The availability and cheapness of photocopying has also increased the amount of charts copied in this way. Although it is not strictly legal, it is becoming commonplace in areas where it is difficult to obtain charts. It was also pointed out by one skipper, that even if one did not have all the necessary charts, it was essential to have all pilot books on board, as a rough sketch plan could always be drawn from the instructions contained in the pilot, if one was faced with navigating through a particular area without charts.

Firearms

The regulations on firearms vary enormously from country to country and cause some problems for voyagers. Firearms are sometimes bonded on board, but more often are removed by the authorities for the duration of the boat's sojourn in port. Among the 100 skippers questioned on this aspect, 38 had firearms on board, but many of them were in two minds over the advisability of carrying a gun while cruising. All skippers, whether having a gun or not, were asked their opinion on this subject and the majority, both among the owners and those without, were firmly against the idea. On the other hand eleven of the owners considered their guns to be essential for their protection. Six skippers who were reluctant to carry arms specified that their possession might be justified in certain parts of the world, even if not in the South Pacific where these interviews took place. Some of the skippers solved this problem by deliberately not sailing to areas with a bad reputation. In the Pacific survey, 21 skippers mentioned that they deliberately avoided Colombia, while others had kept away from certain places in Central America, the Bahamas and West Indies. Several owners regarded their guns as a deterrent, a way of giving peace of mind to the crew or simply as a psychological prop. The most unexpected thumbs down came from André Fily, the skipper of *Stereden Vor*, who used to be a high ranking Gendarme officer, but did not carry a gun and considered them more trouble than they were worth. Because of the various disadvantages of having firearms on board, several boats carried tear gas spray containers, as a good alternative means of self defence. As Willy Zech of *Spirit of Cockpit* saw the problem, 'It's far better to have a potential robber crying his eyes out in the cockpit, than to discover you have shot dead the cousin of the local police chief.'

Quarantine regulations make cruising with animals difficult, but nothing would deter Velda and Denny Moore from taking Captain Prospector and Lara wherever they go.

Pets

To have or not to have a pet is a question most people consider very seriously before setting off on a world cruise. Several countries have stringent regulations regarding cruising animals and this is the reason why their number has decreased over the years. Compared to 13 boats having pets in the Cruising survey, only five of the fifty boats surveyed five years later had pets on board. In both surveys, three quarters of all the skippers rated even the idea of having a pet on a boat with a resounding zero. Many of those interviewed pointed out that although they loved animals, they considered it cruel to force an animal to live in the constricted space of a small sailing boat. Ilse Gieseking of *Lou IV* admitted that setting off on a trip around the world with a dog had been a major mistake, because their freedom of movement had been severely restricted in many countries because of their dog. 'Although animals can be very entertaining at sea, when in port they are a nuisance, because they have to stay on board. Despite our love for our poodle Joshi (named after Joshua Slocum), we would never again take a pet on a future voyage, so as to be more independent . . . but thinking about it, perhaps I wouldn't mind a cat . . .'

Indeed, a few people were less adamant about cats than dogs, but even two of the cat owners said that they would not take one on another voyage.

Erick Bouteleux of *Calao* had at least one good reason to like their cat, when he said, 'Our kitten is a positive plus. Since acquiring it in the Marquesas, we've never had to buy any toys for our two kids.'

Erick would certainly have changed his plus rating if I had asked him the same question one month later, when he had to fight to save his boat from sinking in the vicinity of Futuna. Falling off a wave in rough weather, *Calao* had sprung a leak and was taking in a lot of water. The electrical bilge pump could not cope at all with the influx of water, so Erick cut the cooling intake hose and let the engine draw water straight from the bilge. Only then did he have a chance to look at the bilge pump, which he found to be completely clogged with cat's litter.

Sports and Pastimes

The one question landlubbers invariably ask cruising people is how they spend all the free time that such an apparently carefree life offers them. Obviously a lot of time is taken up by routine maintenance work, but even so, there is still a lot of time left to enjoy oneself, so what *do* cruising people do in their spare time?

As to be expected, water related sports are practised by many of those living afloat. Among the one hundred crews questioned about this aspect of cruising, 15 had sailboards and four surfboards with them. Twenty-nine tenders could be rigged for sailing, many of these being on boats with children on board, for whom a sailing dinghy was a perfect means of exploring nearby coves and inlets.

Snorkelling and diving was another favourite pastime, nearly one third of the boats having diving tanks on board, even if some of these were only kept for emergency underwater repair work. Six boats were equipped with air compressors to fill these tanks. In most cases the snorkelling and diving had a specific purpose, either to spear fish or collect shells. Shelling was one of the most popular hobbies, over half the crews being keen collectors, more often the mate than the skipper. Another favourite occupation was photography, most crews attempting to record their voyage either on slides, on 8mm film or, increasingly, on video tape.

Handicrafts, from macramé to wood carving or making jewellery from coral or shells, occupied many people in quiet anchorages, while at sea the favourite pastimes were reading and listening to music.

Away from the supermarkets, a freshly caught fish makes a welcome change for dinner.

Several people I spoke to, however, prefer to look for physical activities off the boat, often exploring the countries they visit. Two boats had small motorcycles in their forepeak, which were used for exploring the interior of places visited and usually it was quite easy to obtain permission to land the motorbikes. The crew of one boat, being keen mountaineers, made cross country hikes wherever possible.

Gunter Gross of *Hägar* had an instant reply when I asked him what sports he practised.

'The only sport I am interested in is girls!'

However, for Einar Einarsson of *Irma*, who is forced to work en route in order to finance the continuation of the voyage, the answer was simple.

'We do nothing in our spare time except rest; we are professional lazy people.'

Gambol's *Unplanned Circumnavigation*

Some people plan their cruise with great care and detail, while others just let things happen. In Fiji, I came across Stuart Clay who was completing a circumnavigation he had not planned to make. He told me of the haphazard

Gambol sailing slowly into Suva harbour at the end of a six year long circumnavigation.

way this had come about and how, after six years of adventures, he had finally crossed his outward track.

A farmer from Tipuki in New Zealand, Stuart had always been a sailing man, and most weekends would leave his cattle and sheep to go sailing . He had owned a variety of boats, but decided that his eighth and largest, *Gambol*, was just the job to take him farther afield, so he gave up farming and entered *Gambol* for the Auckland to Suva race. He finished in the middle of the fleet, but was happy with his new boat, a sturdy 37 footer, built of strip plank sheathed in fibreglass, so he decided to carry on cruising for a while. One of his crew also chose to stay and the two men spent ten months exploring the many islands of the Fijian archipelago.

Instead of returning home, they sailed via the New Hebrides and New Caledonia to Brisbane, arriving only two days before the great floods that struck the area. Concerned about his uninsured boat, Stuart arranged to have *Gambol* taken out onto the relatively dry shore, but even so the waters rose over the banks, threatening to float her out of the improvised cradle.

MAP D Track of *Gambol*'s Circumnavigation

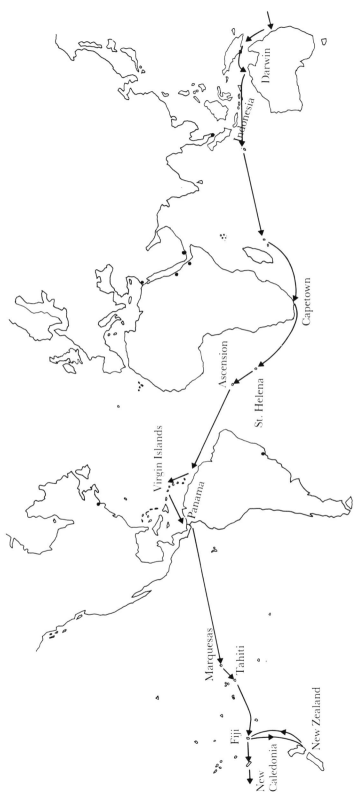

When it was all over, Stuart entered *Gambol* in the Brisbane to Gladstone race, again crossing the finishing line in the middle of the fleet. By now both skipper and crew were broke, so they sailed on to Townsville and worked for nearly a year as deckhands on a dredge to replenish the kitty. Partly cruising and stopping to work periodically, Stuart made his way up inside the Great Barrier Reef to Cooktown, where his crew opted for life ashore. He found an Australian crew and sailed on to Darwin, where there was plenty of work and money to be made, rebuilding the town devastated by a cyclone that had hit the previous Christmas.

Soon *Gambol* was on the move again, sailing across from Darwin to cruise the Indonesian archipelago from Timor to Bali. Planning however is not one of Stuart's stronger points, so he found he was cruising in the wrong season with the North West monsoon in full swing. When the mainsail tore to shreds and the engine blew up, he realised he couldn't carry on and headed back to Darwin. It was back to laying bricks until a new mainsail and engine were paid for.

Having put *Gambol* back into good shape, Stuart took on a new crew and set sail across the Indian Ocean. It was easier to keep going west then to head back home to windward across the notorious Tasman Sea. In Mauritius, Stuart met a South African businessman, who among other things told him to look out for his daughter in Durban. By chance Stuart ran into her the very first day he was ashore and that was the end of male crews on board *Gambol*. Pamela Church joined the cruise in South Africa, has been with Stuart ever since, although now she is Mrs Clay.

In March 1977, Stuart and Pamela left Capetown bound for the Caribbean. They called in at St Helena, but disaster nearly struck on the next leg to Ascension. All day long they had been sailing among a large school of whales, who seemed happy to keep them company, gamboling around the boat, sounding and surfacing near them. Night fell, a dark night, and *Gambol* was running along swiftly doing seven knots with main and boomed genoa wing and wing. Stuart came on watch at midnight and took over the wheel. A few minutes later there was a loud thump and the boat came to an abrupt halt, then she put her nose down, came up, and seconds later was moving again. A big bang like a retort followed, then absolute quiet. The impact had been sudden but soft, so Stuart knew instantly that they had not hit a log, yet the shock made the engine covers and floor boards shoot up into the air. On inspection, Stuart found no structural damage to *Gambol*, only a slight leak in the forward section near to the head. He is certain that they had hit a whale and that the second bang was caused by the whale sounding in fright and hitting them with its tail. Checking the hull later on, he found a few cracks in the fibreglass sheathing and a cracked plank, but nothing serious. Stuart still thanks his lucky star to have been in a strongly built boat and to have escaped with just 'a hell of a fright'.

The rest of their trip to Barbados was uneventful, but soon after arrival they made straight for St Thomas in the Virgin Islands to look for work, as Stuart was flat broke once again. 'It is the story of my life.'

They both found jobs with the big charter boats, painting and varnishing for four dollars a day, then Stuart landed a job as a skipper with the bareboat charter fleet based in Tortola in the British Virgin Islands. It was a sweet job with little work, briefing people on the bareboats they were going to charter. The same company, CSY, later appointed Stuart instructor in the local sailing school. Twenty months were spent there, Pamela and Stuart enjoying every moment of it. Work had not always been so pleasant and neither had it been easy to find on his way around the globe. Having left home with a few months' cruise in mind, not years as it turned out, Stuart had been obliged to work as he went along to finance his cruising.

Eventually he got itchy feet again, so in 1979 he left the Virgin Islands, set sail for Panama and the wide Pacific. In Suva, Stuart completed the 45,000 miles long circumnavigation, that he had never planned, but then planning is not exactly the kind of stuff that men like Stuart are made of. Still, I could not resist asking him about his future plans. He recounted how he hoped to set sail again, but would like to look for a larger boat, around 50 ft, large enough to take paying passengers, who would finance the cruise. The guests would get food, accommodation and a chance to see the world, while Stuart would not have to run around looking for work ashore. Ideally his next boat would be steel and I am sure he had the experience with the whale in the back of his mind when he specified that.

Stuart may not always plan, but this time he certainly kept to his ideas, for two years later he bought the Hiscocks' *Wanderer IV*, a 50 ft steel ketch, with which the Clays are now cruising the South Pacific.

CHAPTER FOUR

Aspects of Seamanship

Boat design, construction materials, rigs and instruments have radically changed over the years, and even some old established concepts of seamanship have come under scrutiny. The sea, however, is unchanging and still challenges the ocean voyager. Contrary to the romantic view that only the sailors of yesteryear were true seamen, from the discussions I have had over the years with many outstanding voyagers, I am convinced that standards of seamanship have not deteriorated and that the majority of cruising skippers treat the sea with due respect. The question of seamanship formed the core of my Cruising survey, when I examined in detail how skippers dealt with emergencies and unforeseen circumstances. In order to find out if there had been any marked changes in this field due to the introduction of new equipment and stronger materials, the same issues were investigated five years later in the Pacific survey.

The combined experiences of the one hundred long distance skippers were indeed considerable, many of them having been sailing all their lives. The interviews gave me the opportunity to tap their wealth of knowledge, acquired by first hand experience, in such matters as heavy weather techniques, dealing with emergencies and other problems at sea.

Heavy Weather

Heavy weather tactics formed a major part of each survey and I asked each skipper when and how he hove to, at what force of wind he would consider laying a-hull or running before the weather, either with storm sails or under bare poles.

Depending on the direction of the wind and having sufficient searoom, most skippers specified that they would carry on sailing in winds up to and including Force 7. With a wind forward of the beam or with land too close for comfort to leeward, most boats would heave to when the wind reached Force 6. Several skippers specified that they hove to not only when the weather deteriorated, but also to slow down, to await daylight for a landfall, or in the

The Beachcomber anchorage in Tahiti.

case of a singlehander without selfsteering, just to rest.

Obviously the techniques of heaving to under sail depended very much on the characteristics and attitude of each boat, as well as on the rig. Thirteen skippers told me that they preferred heaving to under mainsail alone, either full when the wind was not too strong, or reefed. On another ten boats a small foresail was used in combination with the mainsail. Seven ketches usually hove to under a small foresail and mizzen, often reefing the mizzen. Even the skippers who did not rate a ketch too highly as a cruising rig, considered a mizzen sail to be an advantage when heaving to in heavy weather, as it was much easier to deal with than the mainsail. The skipper of one ketch who once hove to under deeply reefed mainsail in extremely rough conditions, found that the solid water breaking over the boat did not have sufficient room to run off under the main boom. He changed to staysail and reefed mizzen, which immediately improved the situation. The skippers of two boats chose to heave to under foresail alone, while one ketch normally hove to under mizzen alone and one schooner under jib and fore-staysail. The skippers of seven boats had never or rarely hove to under sail, going straight to laying a-hull when conditions deteriorated. Tony Ray, who sailed around the world on *Ben*

When it comes to heavy weather, Kiwi circumnavigator Tony Ray of *Ben Gunn* is among the increasing number of skippers whose preferred tactic is dropping all sail and laying a-hull.

Gunn, told me that being worried about breaking the large windows on the 29 ft Herreshoff sloop, they stopped heaving to and preferred laying a-hull when the weather deteriorated, reducing the amount of water breaking over the boat when lying in this way.

In the Pacific survey, however, over half the skippers hove to only when the winds reached Force 8. This may be an indication of the improved strength of sail materials, rigging and the general seaworthiness of contemporary craft. In this later survey I found that the two masted boats usually hove to either under staysail and mizzen or staysail and reefed main. Many sloops and cutters hove to under a storm jib and trisail or deeply reefed main, although some skippers preferred to drop the foresail altogether and heave to under trisail or reefed mainsail alone. Others, however, preferred to save wear and tear on their mainsail by heaving to under staysail or storm jib alone.

When hove to under a backed foresail and reefed mainsail, the boat continues to move ahead, although the foresail tries to counteract this. In strong winds this forward movement may cause heavy water to break over the boat and this is when most skippers would consider dropping all sail and either lying a-hull or running before the weather. When lying a-hull most boats take up a position with the wind and waves abeam, while drifting slowly to leeward.

Talking to the skippers who had gone under bare poles either to lay a-hull or to run before the weather, I found that in each case the decision depended very much on the characteristics of the boat, the state of the sea, the physical condition of the crew and often their age too. Six skippers stated that as soon as the wind reached Force 7 and over, they normally dropped all sail and lay a-hull. Some of these were the smaller boats, or those which did not ride well in heavy seas while hove to under sail. The wind strength at which skippers decided to go to bare poles varied, but nearly half of the 100 interviewed had been forced to drop all sail at one time or another, usually in winds of Force 8 and over. Several skippers described laying a-hull as their preferred tactic in worsening weather conditions, often going straight for this course of action rather than heaving to under some sort of sail. One skipper remarked that being older and not in a hurry, they preferred to take it easy once the weather got uncomfortable. Whether because of their age or their experience, several of these skippers told me that in their younger days they would have carried on sailing under similar conditions, but have now reached the conclusion that lying a-hull has much to recommend it. On the other hand, two young skippers, both stating that their boats were stiff and handled very well in heavy weather, carried on sailing in gale force winds, but would consider laying a-hull in winds over 50 knots. The skipper of only one boat stated that he carried on sailing regardless of the strength of the wind, which he actually had done in winds over Force 10. The boat in question, *Duen*, is a heavy displacement double ender meant to take storms in her stride.

The technique of running before the weather rather than lying a-hull appears to be attracting an increasing number of followers. Several skippers in the Pacific survey stated that they would prefer to run before a storm, generally with a storm jib or a staysail, provided they had enough searoom.

Sea anchors or drogues appear to have lost their appeal with most sailors. Even some of the more traditionally minded skippers considered their usefulness as limited and even doubtful. It was significant that not a single skipper among those interviewed in the Pacific survey mentioned the use of a sea anchor in bad weather, although these could still be found on 11 boats in the Cruising survey. Out of those, only four skippers had ever used them, and not always in bad weather. Albert Steele of *Peregrine* was one of the very few skippers using a sea anchor, which he streamed from the stern of his double ended boat.

Some of the skippers of the boats without sea anchors pointed out that if they desperately needed to slow down their boat, they could easily improvise a drag of some sort. With this contingency in mind some boats carried an old car tyre on board, while others had heavy warps available. Bob Miller of *Galatea IV*, who was once caught by a Force 12 storm, trailed a tyre at the end of an 80 ft warp, slowing down the boat from six to four knots without breaking seas over the stern, the boat being easily kept under control all the time. Paul Glaicher of *Spray* was forced to slow down his fast racing boat as soon as the winds approached the 30-knot mark. By trailing warps astern he could slow the boat down to a manageable 6–7 knots.

The principle of slowing down a boat under extreme conditions has been a matter of debate among cruising skippers. Some are of the opinion that one should carry on as fast as possible, attempting to outrun the following seas, while keeping the boat firmly under control and obviously steering by hand. Nevertheless conditions can arise when however fast a boat is moving, she can be overtaken by a following wave. This is what happened to *Sara III* on passage to Panama, when she encountered heavy weather in the Caribbean. A large wave picked up the Swedish 30 foot sloop and projected it forward, causing it to bury its bow and roll over. Fortunately the boat came up with its mast intact but full of water below and in danger of foundering. While she was lying half submerged she rolled over once more, but again escaped with only minor damage. The skipper Christer Fredriksson told me later that he was convinced that *Sara III* was sailing much too fast for those conditions and if they had slowed down earlier, probably their misadventure would not have happened.

The surveys included a wide range of boats of both heavy and light displacement, large and small, with long and fin keels, so it was very difficult to find a common denominator which would have enabled me to draw some general conclusions on the subject of dealing with heavy weather. However, discussing heavy weather techniques with the most experienced skippers, among whom over a dozen had sailed in excess of 50,000 miles, I detected in each of them a profound confidence in the seaworthiness of their boats. Every one of the skippers I spoke to, who had weathered extreme conditions by dropping all sail, laying a-hull, battening down and leaving the boat to look after itself, stressed the wisdom of such an action and found this tactic more satisfactory than trying to battle with the elements.

Dealing with Emergencies

Several boats included in the survey had their fair share of disasters, in practically every case the crew having to deal with these emergencies themselves, rarely being able to call on outside help. The skippers were asked to describe past emergencies of both mechanical and medical natures, as well as their provisions for dealing with such emergencies in the future.

BREAKAGES AND REPAIRS

Dismasting

Probably the most traumatic failure on a sailing boat is being dismasted, so I tried to find out what provisions boats had for a jury rig if they lost their mast. Several skippers pointed out that they would attempt to salvage as much as possible from whatever rigging and spars were left; 28 boats carried a good supply of spare wire and cable clips to be used in such an emergency. Two of the older wooden boats carried back-up wooden spars, one of whose skippers remarked that his boat was virtually covered in potential jury rigging.

Two of the boats surveyed had been dismasted, and had reached port under jury rig. The trimaran *Spaciety* managed to carry on with a shorter mast, while *Jellicle* built a bipod mast from a large sculling oar and two spinnaker poles lashed together. The use of spinnaker or running poles as a potential jury rig was mentioned by several skippers some of whom stressed that, especially on sloops, the poles should not be carried attached to the mast, so as not to lose them as well if the boat is dismasted. For the same reason, the mizzen mast on cruising ketches should be rigged entirely independently of the main mast.

Rigging Failure

The most common major emergency experienced at sea was that of broken standing rigging, the breakage being caused either by metal fatigue, failure of the wire terminals or of the turnbuckles. In all eight cases the repairs were carried out at sea, two of them involving several hours' work at the masthead. Alan Allmark of *Telemark*, who had to replace a broken turnbuckle at sea, pointed out that the repair could have been much easier if all the turnbuckles on his boat had been the same size, as the only spare he carried was of course not the size that broke. Failure of the masthead fitting caused the loss of a backstay on *Spanish Eyes*, while the masthead fitting on *Abuelo III* was wrenched off by the jib furling gear, a short steep swell imparting to the gear a seesawing motion of tremendous force.

Another common failure at sea was broken halyards and many skippers stressed the usefulness of having sufficient spare halyards, not only to double up existing halyards, but also to be used in place of a broken stay or shroud. Three skippers described the scary experience of going aloft in a seaway to replace a halyard, two going up on a bosun's chair, the third climbing in relative comfort on his mast steps. One recommendation was the fitting of an extra block and halyard at the masthead prior to a long passage to avoid such a contingency.

Steering Breakdown

The third most common failure was that of steering cables, especially during long runs downwind. Although in all cases the repair was carried out at sea, the skippers who did not have emergency tillers easily available recognised the advantage of such a back-up system. Possibly an auxiliary tiller could be mounted permanently.

Such a provision would have been very welcome on two boats, which suffered steering damage in heavy weather. *Spanish Eyes* had great difficulty when the steering cable broke, while *Penelope* also had to return to port with emergency steering after the hydraulic system broke on passage. *Keegenoo* broke its tiller after being knocked down by a freak wave in the Bass Straits. Other damage was also sustained, but emergency repairs saw the boat safely into port.

Other boats had also encountered steering problems after extended downwind runs, when the rudders had been working continuously, under selfsteering. *Calao* arrived in Barbados after an eighteen day crossing of the Atlantic with the rudder supported by only one bolt after the lower pintles had sheered off. The electric pump barely managed to check the flow of water gushing into the boat through the slack rudder gland and the skipper, Erick Bouteleux, confessed that there were times when he was convinced that they would never make land. Erick was also distressed by the fact that they saw a flare four days before reaching Barbados, but were unable to turn back in the 25 knot wind, as by now they had to cope not just with the broken rudder but also with a parted forestay; the mast was only held up by the spare jib halyard.

Jocelyn had an equally dramatic arrival in the Marquesas after the rudder was lost altogether during the last few days of the passage from California. The crew managed to keep the boat steering downwind with the aid of an improvised rudder and the selfsteering paddle. With the help of their amateur radio, the crew raised another boat in the Marquesas who came out to rendezvous with them and assisted them safely into Nuku Hiva. *Jellicle* also lost her rudder, but fortunately the transom-hung rudder was secured to the boat with a lanyard, and could be retrieved. *Spray* lost part of its rudder after hitting an unidentified submerged object off Martinique. The boat managed to return to port with the remaining part of the rudder, but the sacrificial point was subsequently moved lower down so as to retain more of the rudder in the event of another collision.

Engine Problems

Engine repairs were one area in which the self-sufficiency of those experiencing mechanical trouble often let them down and they had to call on outside help, although two skippers managed to carry out spectacular repairs while on passage. Royal McInness of *Mac's Opal* manufactured a new water pump shaft to replace the original, which broke when the cooling water inlet was jammed by pumice stone thrown up by volcanic activity near Tonga. Albert Fletcher of *Duen* (the compulsive tool collector) completely overhauled his engine at sea, even replacing the piston rings. Even if most of the skippers in the survey were unable to carry out repairs of such complexity, all those experiencing trouble while on passage or in remote anchorages managed to put things right by themselves.

Whales

Collision with whales is a subject that has received considerable publicity in recent years and although three of the yachts included in the survey had collided with whales, the damage sustained was not serious enough to endanger any of the boats in question. Two collisions occurred at night, *Gambol*'s in the South Atlantic, *Galatea IV*'s in the Bismarck Sea, and although both were sailing fast at the time, their strongly built hulls survived the impact without serious structural damage. The trimaran *Spaciety*, while on passage from California to the Marquesas, was surrounded by a large group of killer whales, one of whom rammed one float and holed it. Fortunately the stability of the trimaran was not badly affected and Larry Pooter managed to patch up the 14-in diameter hole with plywood, wood screws and underwater epoxy. The improvised patch lasted for four months and the day after the repair *Spaciety* logged 200 miles.

TOOLS FOR THE JOB

To deal with all these emergencies and many others, a good supply of tools and spares are essential. Among the 50 skippers who were questioned on this point, 26 described the range of tools they carried on board as good, while 14 skippers admitted that their tools were only adequate. Ten skippers considered their tool supply as excellent, which often meant that they were able to help out the less fortunate skippers who had not had the means or foresight to acquire all necessary tools before setting off. It should be pointed out however that what was considered as a good supply of tools by some skippers would appear less than an adequate minimum to others. Some boats did not even have a vice, while others had a complete workshop either in the fo'c'sle or near the engine room. Generally a very good supply of tools was carried on those boats built or fitted out by their skippers. Several boats also had a range of power tools to be used in conjunction with a generator.

The importance of being able to carry out essential repairs was stressed again and again. Dud Dewey who has had his fair share of work on his 50-year old *Hawk* considered the ability to fix everything on one's boat of paramount importance, regarding it as the main ingredient for one's safety. Alan Allmark of *Telemark* also pointed out that above everything else, anyone planning a long distance voyage should attempt to be totally self-sufficient in putting things right on his own boat.

MEDICAL EMERGENCIES

Less than one third of the 100 crews surveyed had experienced any accidents or emergencies of a medical nature. Several people went so far as to assert that they felt much fitter and healthier than when they had lived on land, particularly those liberated from deskbound jobs.

The commonest accidents were broken bones. On eight boats various bones were broken, from legs, noses, elbows and wrists to cracked ribs. One couple were unfortunate enough to both break bones in their feet within days of each other. Fortunately however most of these breakages occurred in port and were dealt with professionally at a local hospital. In mid-ocean, Nancy Lewis of *L'Orion* caught the full force of the winch handle across her face, which smashed her nose and did a lot of damage. Via the amateur radio she spoke to the Honolulu medical centre in Hawaii, the amateur network being able to call on specialist advice 24 hours a day. Within ten minutes of the accident she was talking to a neurosurgeon, who advised her exactly what to do. Although on reaching port Nancy had to fly back to the United States for surgery, she is convinced that the excellent advice she received played a major part in the treatment of her injury, which is now not noticeable.

The second commonest problem experienced was serious infection, of various kinds. All of these were dealt with out of the medical chests carried on board. Burns were quite rare: only one person suffered a serious hot water burn, while another nearly lost an eye after welding without wearing goggles. The only serious illness which involved a return to port was pneumonia contracted after the inhalation of vomit during seasickness. Although not described as an emergency, many people mentioned the high incidence of bacterial infections in the tropics and the constant vigilance necessary to prevent cuts and scratches from turning septic. Many of these infections are caused by the staphylococcus bacteria, which once in the blood stream is very difficult to eradicate and may need antibiotic treatment.

In the Cruising survey, I asked all fifty skippers how they would deal with three hypothetical emergencies, namely broken bones, grave burns and appendicitis. In order to deal with broken limbs, twenty one boats carried a selection of splints, two had inflatable splints; while four boats carried a selection of plaster bandages. Eighteen skippers specified that they could easily improvise splints from existing material on board, such as pencils, rulers and sail battens, whereas five boats had no provision for broken bones at all.

Forty-five boats carried specific ointments and/or special sterile burn dressings in their medical chests to deal with grave burns. One skipper stated that he would prefer to leave a burn untreated until he could reach qualified attention, while another skipper recommended jumping in the sea. This is not quite as crazy as it sounds, for one of the priorities in dealing with a major burn is to cool the skin with cold water and clean sea water will do, if fresh water is not readily available. The two big dangers if a burn is serious are infection, and the loss of fluid leading to shock. One boat did carry an intravenous drip for this contingency. Four boats however had no provision for treating a burn.

Appendicitis is an emergency that worries most voyagers and among those interviewed ten people had had their appendix removed before leaving home so as to free themselves of this concern. However the majority of skippers said they would try and temporarily suppress the appendicitis with large doses of antibiotics until they reached port and these thirty-five skippers carried a selection of antibiotics in their medical chests for this purpose. Three skippers were prepared to operate in an emergency. One skipper said that if antibiotics failed to suppress appendicitis in his children he would not hesitate to operate, while another skipper possessed a book, which described the operation step by step. The third skipper was the only one of these with any medical training, being a dentist, and he carried anaesthetic and instruments on his boat for this contingency.

Alain Plantier of *Madame Bertrand* had a taste of what every sailor fears when he went down with suspected appendicitis on a deserted island in Las Perlas off the coast of Panama. The skipper of another boat in the anchorage described his symptoms and what antibiotics they had available to a doctor in Venezuela, contacted via the amateur radio. The Venezuelan amateur also contacted Panama, where a helicopter was put on standby by the US Navy. The antibiotic course suggested by the doctor brought about a marked improvement and a few days later Alain was taken back to Panama, where it was decided that an operation was not necessary.

Among the 100 crews questioned on the subject of medical emergencies and preparedness, on half the boats someone, or sometimes several of the

Advanced First Aid Afloat is one of the manuals found on many cruising boats. Its author, Dr Peter Eastman, and his wife Betty, who have made cruising their way of life, featured in both the Suva and Pacific surveys.

crew, had taken a First Aid course. On 12 boats such a course was not applicable as the crews had the necessary knowledge from their profession in the medical field as doctors, dentists, nurses or pharmacists. Those people who had amateur radio on board invariably stated that they would seek qualified advice through the amateur radio networks. Most boats carried a first aid manual, often *Advanced First Aid Afloat*, whose author, Dr. Peter Eastman, and his boat *Con Tina* have featured in two of these surveys. In his mid-seventies and still actively cruising, Dr. Eastman is a walking advertisement for the healthy nature of the cruising life.

A similar preparedness was seen in the medical supplies included in the medical chest. On 40 boats these were described as comprehensive or even excellent, on 54 they were considered adequate and only six skippers thought they had just the minimum.

Obviously for ocean voyaging the medicine chest should contain a wide variety of medicines. A basic list for an extended cruise away from immediate medical facilities should include at least the following:

Cotton wool
Various sizes of waterproof adhesive dressings

Sterilised lint

Bandages

Crepe bandages for sprains

Special sterile dressings for burns

Scissors, forceps, safety pins

Thermometer

Disposable syringes and needles

Sterile needles with sutures for stitching

Disinfectant

Antiseptic solution or ointment

Antibiotic powder (eg containing neomycin, powder may be better than creams under moist tropical conditions)

Cream or spray for treatment of burns (antibiotics, phenergan)

Antihistamine cream to relieve insect bites and stings

Antihistamine anti-allergic tablets (which can be used for allergies to food, insect bites, jelly fish stings etc.)

Antibiotics – ampicillin (covers a wide range of infections, available as a syrup for children)
– tetracycline (not recommended under 12 years, large doses can suppress appendicitis in an emergency)

Sulphonamide antibacterial, for urinary tract infections

Laxative

Antidiarrhoeal tablets or kaolin mixture for children

Analgesic – aspirin/paracetamol for minor pain, also for reducing temperature
– pentazocine for more severe pain

Sleeping tablets, useful for helping someone in severe pain to get a good night's sleep

Promethazine elixir, such as phenergan, useful as a sedative for a sick child and also for allergic conditions, nausea, etc.

Local anaesthetic to allow cleaning and stitching of a major wound

Specific local anaesthetic drops for removing foreign bodies from the eye

Drops and ointments for eye infections (chloramphenicol)

Ear drops for bacterial ear infections

Antifungal preparations for athletes foot and other fungal infections

Antiseasickness tablets

Insect repellant

Sun screen lotion

Antimalarial tablets for prophylactic use

Medical advice should be sought as to which antibiotics to take, as some people are sensitive to penicillin and like all powerful drugs, antibiotics should not be used lightly. Many people carry disposable syringes and needles in case they have to have an injection in countries which do not use disposables, as the risk of hepatitis from improperly sterilised needles and syringes is considerable.

The danger of using antibiotics without proper advice was highlighted when Mac Macauley of *Acheta* had an attack of hepatitis while anchored near a remote island 70 miles off the coast of Mexico. Although describing his symptoms over the amateur radio, they received the wrong medical advice, being told that Mac should take tetracycline, an antibiotic which in fact should not be used where liver or kidney ailments are suspected. As a result, Mac got steadily worse and finally his wife June decided to up anchor and singlehand *Acheta* back to the mainland, where a doctor diagnosed hepatitis and prescribed the proper treatment.

In recent years there has been a resurgence of malaria in many tropical countries and it is highly recommended to start taking the prophylactic drugs before entering a known malarial area. Information on these areas can be obtained from local health authorities, who will also recommend the appropriate drug to take, as some strains of malaria have now become resistant to some of these drugs.

Regulations regarding drugs vary enormously from country to country and some customs officials confiscate certain drugs, such as strong painkillers like morphine. In several countries however, the laws are very relaxed, and drugs that normally need a prescription, such as antibiotics, can be bought over the counter. Many boats use this opportunity to stock up their medical chest or replace drugs which are past their expiry date. In fact several skippers stressed the importance of renewing medicines regularly, especially antibiotics, as their effectiveness decreases with age and storage in tropical conditions.

For those wishing to be able to consult an English speaking doctor in case of an emergency abroad, the International Association for Medical Assistance to Travellers can be of help in more than 140 countries. It is possible to obtain a list of doctors on the IAMAT register by writing to one of its offices. Although membership is free, a small donation is usually welcome. These doctors charge set fees for card holding members, which are often lower than in most Western countries. Some addresses of IAMAT are:

736 Center St, Lewiston, NY 14092, USA
188 Nicklin Rd, Guelph, Ontario N1H7L5, Canada

Seasickness is an ongoing problem and a surprisingly high number of voyagers suffer from it to a lesser or greater extent, the proportion of women being much higher than that of men. On nearly one third of the boats there was at least one person suffering from seasickness, if only for the first few days after a long spell in port. Several of the children complained about seasickness, although as they did not have to play a part in the sailing of the boat, they just lay down until they felt better. Many of those suffering only partial seasickness took no drugs, but among those who did take something, the most successful appear to be either Stugeron or the Transderm patch. This patch is put behind the ear and gradually emits the drug scopolamine, which acts by deadening the nerves of the inner ear. In one case, two patches were used successfully by a person who in the past used to be extremely sick. In most cases the Transderm patch was only worn for a few days until the crew had found his or her sea legs.

A major problem which causes some concern to voyagers in tropical waters is *ciguatera*. This type of fish poisoning is found among fish caught close inshore and near reefs and rarely applies to fish caught by trolling in the open ocean. There is at present no way to detect a toxic fish and toxicity varies from island to island and from species to species. For this reason many crews preferred not to fish at all. Others took the advice of local people, on which fish were edible and which section of a reef to avoid.

Several crews I spoke to had suffered from *ciguatera* intoxications, some of them being left sensitive and unable to eat fish without a recurrence of the symptoms. One of these, a doctor, said he should have known better than to eat moray eel, which is one of the species most likely to be toxic. The symptoms are unpleasant, usually gastrointestinal. There are also particular neurological symptoms such as tingling and numbness. It can be fatal in rare cases and severe attacks can leave the victim weak for months.

Ciguatera has been a mystery illness in the Caribbean and Pacific since it was first described by Columbus, but more about what causes these outbreaks is now becoming known, mainly due to the research team led by Dr. Bagnis in Tahiti. He has shown that it is caused by a tiny one-celled plant, which grows on coral and is eaten by fish. These organisms grow quickly on any exposed coral surface and Dr. Bagnis has shown how outbreaks of *ciguatera* have followed natural destruction of the coral (such as the outbreak which followed tidal waves and violent storms in the Marquesas in the 1960s or man-induced destruction, such as blasting, dredging, dumping, construction of quays and breakwaters.

The toxin is cumulative and most likely to affect people who rely on fish to form a major part of their diet, as did several of these voyagers who were on tight budgets. However a large number of areas and fish are trouble free and fresh fish is a tasty dinner sought after by many cruising people, so a few pointers might be helpful. Trolling in the open sea is fairly safe. Of the reef fish, surgeon and parrot fish are most likely to be toxic, also any of the large predators such as snapper, barracuda and grouper. Those over 30 inches may have accumulated toxin and should be avoided. The liver, roe and head should not be eaten and care taken not to puncture the intestines when cleaning. In doubtful areas it is prudent not to eat fish more than once or twice a week and preferably in small portions, as the toxicity is directly related to the amount eaten. Local knowledge is usually reliable.

Unfortunately there is no specific treatment for *ciguatera*, although the intravenous injection of calcium glutonate with Vitamins B_6 and B_{12} has had some success, apparently acting to prevent the passage of the toxins into the cells.

Another serious condition for which there is no treatment and which can also be contracted from food or drink is tropical meningitis. This is caused by a parasite which is ingested, possible with unwashed vegetables or salad, and which makes its way into the brain. Hugh Brown of *Nightwing* contracted this meningitis in Fiji and was extremely ill for a month. Although flying to New Zealand for diagnosis, Hugh still had not recovered completely after one year, time being the only healing factor. In contrast to *ciguatera*, where local people are more vulnerable, the local population appears to have some immunity to this eosinophilic meningitis and it was mainly foreigners, whether diplomats, businessmen or yachtsmen, who had been affected in Fiji, sometimes fatally.

The Daily Routine

In both the Cruising and Pacific surveys, there was a section dealing with the day to day running of the ship at sea. Although the two surveys were separated by several years, so many of the earlier findings were confirmed by the later interviews that it was considered logical to merge the data and present the conclusions as a whole.

REDUCING SAIL

Testing their cautiousness, I asked the 100 skippers if and when they considered reducing sail. Eighteen skippers stated that they reduced sail at night as a matter of principle, regardless of the weather, mostly because they were shorthanded. On the other hand, when conditions looked doubtful, whether at night or during the day, 80 skippers said they would start reducing sail, without waiting for the weather to demonstrate its intention. It appeared that most skippers tended to err on the cautious side, rather than be caught with too much sail up. Nevertheless, some of the skippers of the old school pointed out that nowadays they carried sail much longer than they used to, relying on the superior strength of modern materials.

The majority of boats had slab reefing for their mainsails and the switchover to this system was demonstrated by the larger number of boats fitted with it in the Pacific survey (44) compared to the Cruising survey (32). The number of roller reefing gears had dropped from 13 to 2, a system regarded by their owners as less efficient and convenient than slab reefing. On most ketches the mizzen had points reefing, even when the mainsail itself had slab or roller reefing.

The skippers were also asked to comment on the advantages and disadvantages of their particular reefing system. Those having slab reefing were the most satisfied, mainly because of the speed and ease of operation. The average time estimated by the skippers for putting one reef in their mainsails by this method was three to five minutes.

SAFETY HARNESSES

On twelve boats, safety harnesses were worn all the time by any person working on deck, not just the skipper. The crews of an additional twenty boats wore harnesses occasionally, both in good and bad weather. On nineteen boats harnesses were always worn during heavy weather, while on another eight boats harnesses were worn by those on night watch. The skippers of sixteen boats told me that they wore a harness both at night and in heavy weather. On the remaining twenty-five boats safety harnesses were virtually never worn, although in most cases they were available on board.

Two of the skippers had fallen overboard while on passage. Fortunately they were wearing harnesses at the time and managed to climb back on board unaided. Among those who admitted that they never wore a harness, a few reasoned that it restricted their freedom of movement, especially in an emergency situation when action had to be taken quickly, such as when hit by an unexpected squall and all sail had to be dropped in an instant. It was a rule on some boats that the person on watch at night should never leave the cockpit without informing someone else. As a means of making deck work safer, three of the boats had mast pulpits fitted, a safety feature highly praised by its owners.

WATCHKEEPING

The system followed for keeping watches varied enormously from boat to boat, from a few who did not keep regular watches at all to a handful of skippers who run their ships along Navy lines. Two factors greatly influenced the watchkeeping; whether the boat was equipped with selfsteering or automatic pilot, and the number of crew available. Out of the 100 boats, eleven had neither a selfsteering device nor an automatic pilot, six of them being steered by hand continuously and thus being forced to keep a regular system of watches. The crews of the remaining five boats occasionally let the boats look after themselves by trimming the sails and adjusting the tiller. Obviously, the six singlehanders, one of whom had no selfsteering, could not even attempt to keep regular watches, although they tried to keep as good a lookout as possible. This is not always good enough, a fact which is underlined by Jan Swerts' loss of *Tehani III* on a reef in Fiji on a dark night with a heavy sea running. For the previous two days the sky had been overcast and he had been unable to take a sight. The combination of an erroneous DR position and the fact that under these conditions he was unable to keep a permanent lookout, had disastrous consequences.

On most boats where watches were kept as a matter of routine, a fixed system of watches only operated at night. In the case of many couples there was a give and take attitude, often the men taking longer watches at night. On most boats with a crew of two, the nights were split into four three hour periods, with two watch and two rest periods. The boats with a crew of three had a similar arrangement, so that in any given night only one crew member had to take two watches. The boats with larger crews generally kept two hour watches, especially those steered by hand. All the older children took watches, although not always by night, while on one boat without selfsteering, the children had to take day and night watches and steer by hand like everyone else. On another boat, two younger children stood their watch together.

The system of watches was generally altered in the event of bad weather, the skippers of shorthanded boats either reducing the length of the watch or putting the entire crew on standby below with only an occasional lookout being kept in the cockpit. A number of boats, especially those with larger crews, did not change their watchkeeping systems in heavy weather.

Even on boats keeping a loose system of watches most of the time, more careful watches were kept when nearing land or sailing close to known shipping lanes. Seven skippers admitted that while on passage away from shipping lanes no watches were kept at all and the entire crew went to sleep at night. On another seven boats, proper watches were also not kept, the skipper relying on crew members and himself to occasionally wake up and look around, the length of these intervals being of various durations, although on most boats this would be done about once every hour. Several boats, whose skippers insisted that nominal watches were kept, should in fact be included in the latter category as their crews' attitude to the chore of keeping watches was very casual in mid-ocean, the watchkeeper often dozing between lookouts.

These conclusions confirmed the findings of my Suva survey, when the system of watches on long distance boats had also been investigated. Among the 62 boats of that survey, on only 45 was a full system of watches in operation, with all adult members of the crew taking their turn at watchkeeping. The remaining 17 boats, and not necessarily those with smaller crews, kept very loose watches, the crew going to sleep at night when on passage and keeping a minimum of watches at other times.

The lackadaisical approach to watchkeeping was condemned by two skippers, who pointed out that they had often seen shipping at night even outside of known shipping lanes, thus invalidating the arguments of those who see no reason why anyone should try and keep awake if there is no shipping around.

'It is only the people who don't keep watches who never see ships at sea, we seem to meet them all the time,' was the comment of Mike Morrish, who decided to sail *Fortuna* around the world without selfsteering gear for the precise reason of having someone on watch all the time.

LIGHTS AT NIGHT

The showing of lights at night is another point of varying opinion and practice. Half of the skippers stated that when on passage and well offshore their boats showed no lights at all. Only nine boats showed their correct regulation lights at all times, while eight skippers specified that they only had their navigation lights on when in known shipping lanes. However, 38 skippers always showed some kind of light from the masthead, either an all round white, a combined tricolour navigation light, or in the case of four boats, a white flashing strobe light. The remaining boats burned a paraffin light at deck level, although one skipper who used to do this in the past had abandoned the practice and now preferred to show a masthead light after finding that the bright light at deck level disturbed his night vision.

The boats showing electric lights at night were not necessarily those with more generating power available. I also tried to draw a parallel between showing lights and keeping regular watches, as some skippers had mentioned the fact that they always showed a light if no one was on watch. In fact I found that ten of the boats whose crews kept either casual watches or no watches at all at night, also failed to show any lights. The skippers of the other 36 boats who did not normally show a light when on passage, did keep watches and specified that the person on watch would put on the navigation lights as soon as a ship was sighted.

MEAL PATTERNS

While talking about the daily routine on the 50 boats in the cruising survey, I also asked about the number of meals taken in both normal and bad weather. The crews of 35 boats usually ate three meals a day; on thirteen boats only two meals per day would be served, while on two boats the crew would have only one proper meal plus snacks. On most boats the main cooked meal was served in the evening. Several crews reduced the number of meals in the event of heavy weather, relying on lighter meals and frequent snacks. Thirty of these long distance voyagers however carry on having their usual number of meals regardless of weather conditions.

WEATHER FORECASTS

Taking bad weather in his or her stride is very much a characteristic of the seasoned sailor, so it was not a great surprise to hear that of the 82 skippers who generally listen to weather forecasts, only 60 were influenced by them, usually prior to a departure. Eighteen skippers stated that they never listen to forecasts, preferring to interpret themselves the information on hand. But even the skippers who are not normally influenced by the forecasts during the relatively safe sailing season, show more prudence if sailing in tropical areas during the hurricane or cyclone season. Half the skippers stated that they leave the hurricane areas as a matter of course during the bad season. The majority of those who decide to stay attempt to move as little as possible and remain close to a hurricane hole or safe port. Most of them try to listen to the weather forecasts at least once a day, either local or the long range international and regional forecasts. Many tune in regularly to the WWV and WWVH stations, which give continuously updated information on tropical depressions and storms.

The two stations are operated by the United States National Bureau of Standards, WWV being based in Fort Collins, Colorado, while WWVH is based in Kauai, Hawaii. The services offered by the two stations, both of which broadcast continuously, are varied, their time signals and storm warnings being their most important features. Voice announcements are made once every minute, but to avoid confusion, a male voice is used on WWV and female voice on WWVH. The WWVH announcement occurs first, at 15 seconds before the minute, followed by the WWV announcement at 7½ seconds before the minute. Every second is marked by a pulse, with the exception of the 29th and 59th second pulses, which are omitted. The specific hour and minute mentioned are in 'Coordinated Universal Time' (UTC), which is the same as GMT.

Weather information about major storms or tropical depressions in the Atlantic and Eastern North Pacific are broadcast in voice on WWV at 8, 9 and 10 minutes after each hour. Similar warnings covering the Western Pacific Ocean are given on WWVH at 48, 49 and 50 minutes after each hour. An additional minute (the 11th on WWV and the 51st on WWVH) is sometimes used when there are unusually widespread storm conditions. If there are no warnings in the designated area, this will be indicated in the announcement.

A typical warning would have the following format:

'North Atlantic weather West of 35 West at 1700 UTC: Hurricane Donna, intensifying, 24 North, 60 West, moving northwest, 20 knots, winds 75 knots.'

The two stations can also be called up for similar information on the following telephone numbers: WWV on (303) 499-7111 and WWVH on (808) 335-4363.

In several cruising areas there are now amateur radio networks run by landbased enthusiasts, who cater specifically for cruising boats, not only keeping track of their position but also relaying daily weather information. Several skippers mentioned that while on passage they used this information for plotting a more efficient course to take advantage of the existing or impending weather systems. Several skippers, who did not have an amateur licence or transmitter, had bought radio receivers which were capable of tuning in to these amateur bands, for the purpose of listening in to weather information.

Eight of the boats in the Pacific survey had experienced a hurricane first hand, usually at anchor, some having the misfortune to experience more than one. All of these boats now made sure they left the area, but while conducting the interviews in Tahiti, I was surprised how many skippers had chosen to remain in French Polynesia, which has suffered several disastrous cyclones in recent years. Indeed some of them had the local radio on all the time, while others said they expected to find out from their neighbours who did listen to WWVH if a hurricane was on its way.

One question I asked all the skippers in the Pacific survey was if they thought their boats could survive a full hurricane at sea. Just over half were convinced that their boats would see them through, while others either did not know or would put all hope in their lucky stars. Denny Moore of *Prospector* was convinced that '. . . over 100 knots, ninety per cent of survival is pure luck'. Several skippers thought that even if their boats would survive a hurricane, they were not so sure that they and their crew could.

ASTRO-NAVIGATION

While on passage and well offshore, the navigators on 66 boats (who were not always the skipper) relied on two sun sights a day for plotting their position. In most of these cases the position was worked out from a morning line of position transferred to a noon sight, whereas the remaining navigators generally prefer to transfer the noon latitude to an afternoon sight. On 24 boats the navigators took three sights (morning, noon and afternoon) as a matter of routine, while the navigator of another boat took six sights daily, admitting that as an ex-pilot he took so many sights mainly for pleasure. On five boats the navigators had little use for the noon sight, plotting their position by transferring a morning line of position to an afternoon sight, while on six boats astro-navigation was limited to a daily meridian altitude giving latitude, the longitude being obtained by applying the course and distance run to the noon position. A few skippers pointed out that while in mid-ocean, they took sights only on alternate days, possibly updating their positions from the distance run. Several skippers stated that they found it sufficient to work out their accurate position only once every 48 hours. Nearing landfall, on the other hand, more than half the navigators increased the number of sights taken, often using other celestial bodies as well as the sun. The remaining boats carry on as before, with an average of two sights per day, although their skippers said that they would keep a more alert watch. Gunter Gross of *Hägar*, who has a healthy regard for the many reefs in the South Pacific, told me that when nearing landfall he uses his sextant until it runs hot.

Although relying mostly on the sun for their sights, most navigators occasionally used other celestial bodies in their calculations. For example, 54 navigators had occasionally used the moon, even if some of them extremely rarely, while the rest had never even attempted to shoot the moon. A similar proportion would occasionally use the stars or planets, with only a few navigators taking star sights routinely.

On discussing astro-navigational problems, I found that the sight reduction tables No 249 (AP 3270 in the UK) were most popular, being used by 73 per cent of the navigators. Less popular were tables No 229 (NP 401 in the UK) used only by 16 per cent of those interviewed.

Most navigators choose the Sight Reduction Tables for their simplicity in working out a sight. As a matter of personal preference more navigators in the Suva survey used the Sight Reduction Tables for Air Navigation (HO249) rather than those destined for marine navigation (HO229). The former consists of only three volumes, each covering 30° of latitude, whereas the latter consists of six volumes. The method of calculation for both tables is similar, both being used in conjunction with the Nautical Almanac for the current year. On twelve boats a navigational computer was used for various calculations in astro-navigation, one of their main advantages being that they

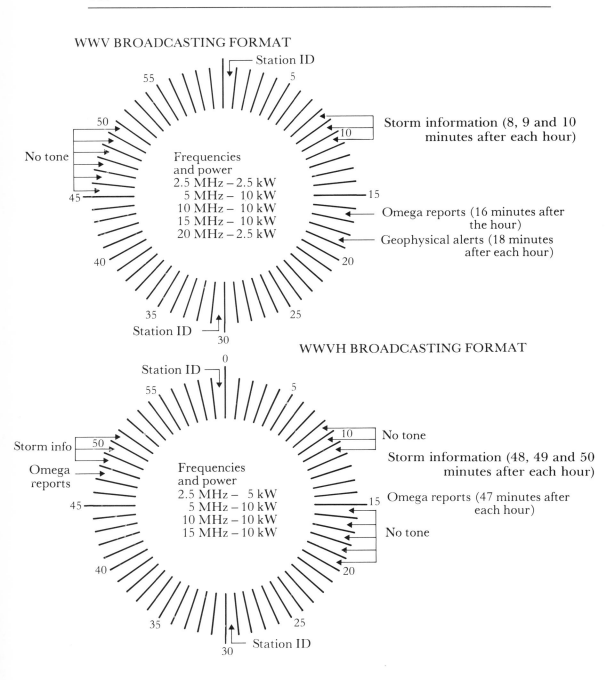

DIAGRAM 1 *The hourly broadcasting schedules of WWV and WWVH*

Canadian singlehander Dick Thuillers of *Because* positively enjoys navigation and takes many sights daily for this reason.

store all data contained in the Nautical Almanac until well into the next century.

The proliferation of SatNavs on cruising boats has resulted in a marked change in the offshore navigation routine on many boats. Over half the boats in the Pacific survey were equipped with SatNav, and 19 skippers among these stated that they had been greatly influenced by it. Six navigators even admitted that because of SatNav they had given up astro-navigation completely. Among the SatNav owners the majority used their sextants much less than before, some of them only to keep their hands in or to check the accuracy of the SatNav, or rather vice versa.

Mac Macauley of *Acheta* said that SatNav had given him confidence in his sextant work as the results could be compared immediately, while Jamie Bryson of *Ave del Mar* admitted that SatNav had made him realise that he was not as competent as he had thought he was. A few skippers were using SatNav in this way to improve the accuracy of their astro-navigation.

Among the SatNav users there were several who tried not to be influenced by it and still always cross-checked with a sextant at least once a day. Those who enjoyed astro-navigation carried on taking sights regardless, such as Bill Smith of *Jenelle*, who took at least six sights a day as a matter of course. Also following his pre-SatNav routine, Joe McKeown of *Shanachie* ran two plots on his charts, one based on celestial, the other on satellite navigation, aware that SatNavs have sometimes packed up.

SUGGESTIONS

After listening to so many tales of the dangers that lie in wait for the unwary sailor, and the valuable lessons the skippers had learnt from dealing with every kind of emergency, I concluded each interview by asking for their views on how cruising could be made safer for those who intend to follow in their wake. This was the only point at which skippers were asked to make general comments and to answer specific questions, which resulted in a wide variety of valuable suggestions being made.

On the question of seamanship in general, it was stressed again and again that good seamanship begins in port with sound preparations for the intended voyage. Nevertheless, only a quarter of the skippers thought that overall safety at sea could simply be improved by having better boats with better gear, and even fewer thought that an improvement in safety could be achieved by better instruments. Although an improvement in the quality of boats and gear could make some difference, all skippers agreed that the final key to safety was the crew themselves. According to Charles Pickering of *Keegenoo*, 'There is already plenty of good equipment available, but it is the crews that let the boats down, rather than the boat letting the crew down. Even when we were knocked down in the Bass Straits, it was probably my own fault that it happened.'

This is a view shared by Bernard Tournier of *Volte*, who stressed the importance of being aware of the risks when one puts to sea. 'Cruising is not necessarily dangerous, in most cases the dangers are created by one's own errors.'

Experience in this respect obviously counts and many skippers pointed out that experienced crews rarely get into real trouble and therefore one should attempt to learn as much as possible about the sea, both in practice and in theory, before leaving home waters.

Paul Glaicher thought that as so many of the present boats are crewed by couples, cruising could be made a lot safer if the women on board became more proficient, knowing how to deal with all aspects of sailing, from navigation to sail trimming. He spoke from the fortunate position of having as his partner on *Spray* Dana Nicholson, a professional yacht skipper of considerable offshore experience.

The importance of experience was also mentioned by Alain Plantier of

Madame Bertrand, who agreed that although cruising safety depended on the quality of boat and equipment, just as much as on the quality of the skipper, '. . . those who are experienced would make a better choice of boat in the first place'.

Several skippers agreed that some of the latest gear can contribute greatly to make cruising safer, such as furling jibs, stronger sail materials, SatNavs or amateur radios. However, this reliance should not be allowed to go too far, because as Larry Schneider of *Moli* pointed out, 'some people put too much faith in electronics and when these fail, they don't know what to do'.

The danger of focussing all one's energy and attention on a non-essential matter in an emergency was underlined by Denny Moore of *Prospector*, who gave as an example the fate of the crew of *Summer Sea*. During cyclone *Reva* in the Tuamotus, Denny had heard them over the radio describing their inability to deal with a faulty engine, which was occupying all their attention to the point of obsession. Their lack of attention to the rest of the boat in those critical moments ended in disaster as the airwaves went silent and the boat and crew were lost.

Hugh Brown of *Nightwing* also considered this tendency to rely on gear rather than on one's own devices to be dehumanising. 'People should rather strive to develop their sea sense and learn to rely more on their own senses.'

Discussing specific aspects of seamanship, several skippers, Eric Hiscock among them, pointed out that nowadays people tended to rely too much on engines and engine power. This was a conclusion that could also be drawn from my Suva survey, when the majority of the skippers stressed the importance of having a reliable and powerful energy source at their disposal. According to another veteran sailor, Mike Bailes of *Jellicle*, this reliance on auxiliary power sometimes means that boats find themselves in dangerous situations, such as being anchored too near a potential leeshore, motoring too close to a reef under calm conditions, or tied up to a dock with an onshore wind.

Yet, in spite of these valid criticisms, the majority of today's sailors would consider cruising without an engine an inconceivable proposition. There is indeed little doubt that engines make cruising more agreeable, often enabling one to get into places, or out of them, which are denied to the engineless boat.

Burghard Pieske, of *Shangri-La*, pointed out that without an engine they would have been in great trouble in Le Maire Strait, in the vicinity of Cape Horn. The combination of opposing tide, strong ocean current and wind produced frightening conditions which the crew described as a witches' cauldron. The sails were slatting so badly in the violent swell that they were threatening to bring down the mast rigging. Burghard felt that even a strongly built catamaran like *Shangri-La* could have been broken up under such conditions, if they had not had sufficient power to motor out of trouble.

Opinions on seamanship may have changed with time, but most basic rules seem to have remained the same. I found that even the most experienced sailors among those interviewed were not dogmatic and indeed were ready to accept new ideas. Even so, one skipper remarked that there was still a lot to be learned by reading and re-reading the books of oldtimers like Slocum and the rest. The unpretentiousness of those oldtimers and their respect for the sea were reflected by many of those interviewed, who described their achievements and experiences with modesty and frankness. The major conclusion to be drawn from talking to such a variety of outstanding sailors is that good seamanship ultimately depends on one's own mental attitude. Mike Bailes, who has spent most of his life at sea, best summed this up by saying that above everything else one must learn to be patient.

Mike Bailes and Jellicle—Simplicity Perfected

On the grassy sward behind the quay at Port Vila, the capital of Vanuatu, a dozen New Hebrideans sat in a circle, exercise books on their laps, listening with rapt attention to a thin man with a bushy blond beard holding forth in fluent Bislama. My first glance around any new port is to see if there is anyone there whom I know, but I could not have been more delighted than meeting this man again. He saw me, interrupted his discourse and greeted me warmly.

'Well, Mike, what are you up to this time?' I asked. He explained that he was giving lessons in seamanship and basic navigation to local fishermen and sailors. In the two months since arriving in Port Vila he had mastered Bislama, a pidgin language, which is widely used in this part of the Pacific.

'I just bought the New Testament in Bislama and read it out aloud a few times. I soon got the feel of the language as most of its words are taken from English.' Mike found that neither the French nor the British administration, who ran the joint colony, had done anything to give formal training to the sailors working on local vessels. Being well qualified for the job as an ex-officer of the Royal Navy, Mike set about filling this demand himself.

Although I had questioned Mike Bailes for one of my surveys, when we had met previously in Tuvalu, I was so fascinated by the man and the wisdom he had to impart, that I set my taperecorder rolling and over a bottle of French wine I persuaded him to recount the story of his life.

For the last twenty years Mike has been roaming the oceans in *Jellicle*, a 25 ft Folkboat named after the T. S. Eliot cat that danced in the moonlight. *Jellicle* is simple to the point of being spartan. Mike has no use for an engine, instead preferring a sweep and full set of sails kept in tip top condition. Below deck,

After many years on *Jellicle*, Mike Bailes would not change his spartan Folkboat for anything.

amidst coils of rope, baskets and sacks of basic provisions are two bunks, a navigation table and a simple primus stove. The oldtimers like Joshua Slocum are Mike's mentors and he aims to keep his life as simple as theirs with little time for luxuries. He wouldn't swap *Jellicle* for anything larger or more modern, however much money he had. Mike likes his small Folkboat, which he can sail like a dinghy, but also because it makes him feel closer to the sea he loves and respects.

'Someone once gave me some nice stainless steel cleats, but I took them off after a while and put the old wooden ones back on again. They just spoilt the look of *Jellicle*.' Shiny metal would certainly look out of place on such a basic boat, with no lifelines, a boarded over cockpit to keep out the water and solid wooden spars.

Mike's love for the sea has been with him all his life. His claim to fame that he jokingly boasts about is to be the first officer in the history of the Royal Navy to be courtmartialled twice, found guilty on both occasions, yet still to retire honourably as a Lieutenant Commander on a full pension. The first incident occurred when he was first officer on a submarine and involved in developing a fast turbine engine using a new fuel. His briefcase containing all classified documents relating to the new engine disappeared while Mike was having a few drinks with his fellow officers at a pub near the Admiralty in

London. Mike and his commanding officer were found guilty of negligence at a court martial, but were not punished too severely.

From fast submarines, Mike turned his attention to survival in ships' lifeboats, trying to prove that long voyages in such open boats could still be accomplished, as Captain Bligh had so aptly demonstrated. After a few shorter voyages sponsored by the Navy, Mike selected a crew for a transatlantic voyage. Plans were well advanced when at the last moment the top brass cancelled the voyage as being too risky. Mike accepted the decision as any good officer would and so did his crew, except for a young Scotsman, who had also been Mike's crew in his first lifeboat. Utterly dejected and distressed by another ten years in the Navy, the young man threatened to commit suicide. Feeling responsible for the man's plight, Mike wrote to him advising him to desert rather than take his own life. The letter was found and Mike found himself in prison, facing yet another court martial for inciting a rating to desert. Again he was found guilty, although the board was understanding enough to realise that he had acted in good faith and no punishment was exacted.

Mike however had already reached the decision that he had had enough of

Sailing without an engine, Mike Bailes tries never to find himself in a situation that he cannot sail out of. For this reason *Jellicle* is equipped with a wide inventory of sails.

the Navy and when the opportunity arose two years later, he retired honourably and with a pension. He bought *Jellicle*, not much bigger than a ship's lifeboat, and set off to show that long ocean passages in such a boat were perfectly feasible.

Mike Bailes now considers the vast Pacific to be his home, for in *Jellicle* he has covered over 100,000 miles over the years sailing back and forth to every island group south of the Equator. Speaking several Pacific languages, Mike is often to be found in the local library reading books on Pacific history. For several years he made his base in Tonga, running a marine school for young Tongans and commanding a local trading vessel from time to time. Bringing back forgotten skills to a new generation of seafaring islanders gave him both satisfaction and a worthwhile occupation.

For the last few years Mike has often taken on as crew Pacific islanders, teaching them the art of sailing in a practical way. One of his first crew, known to everyone as Tonga Bill, caught the bug of cruising and built his own 18-footer from second-hand timber and empty crates salvaged from the Auckland docks. After sailing in the Pacific for several years, Bill has since set off across the Indian Ocean, determined to be the first Tongan navigator to circle the globe. Mike's next disciple, Pita Filitonga, was qualified enough at the age of eighteen to be the navigator on a traditional canoe sailing thousands of miles from Vanuatu to Papua New Guinea for the Pacific Festival of Arts. The last time I met Mike in New Zealand, he was talking of sailing to visit Pita in Australia, as if crossing the Tasman Sea was like visiting friends in the next village. Alternatively he might sail again to Vanuatu, from where he had recruited his latest crew member, Wari Farea.

'I never have girls as crew,' laughs Mike, 'I find them too distracting,' and he launched into a story about how he nearly lost an expensive charter schooner in the Caribbean, when both he and his first mate were head over heels about the same girl in the crew. Too much in love to think straight, he once let the boat go too near a reef, was unable to go about, and ran aground. It never occurred to him to start the engine; he just watched it all happen in slow motion. Ironically, the Royal Navy frigate which came to the rescue was commanded by an ex-colleague, who laughingly told Mike, 'Fortunately, no court martial for you this time, Commander Bailes.'

After that episode, Mike has banned women from his ship, except as visitors in port.

'No woman would live this frugally anyway,' Mike added with a smile, as he watched my wife Gwenda casting an eye over *Jellicle*'s uninviting interior. While living modestly and frugally, Mike still enjoys life and lives it to the full. He has a great ability to get on with people and is an extremely patient teacher, a quality much appreciated by the islanders. Anyone can learn a lot from him, especially about the virtues of patience and simplicity for those whose lives are involved with the sea.

The morning I left Port Vila, I met Mike walking along the main street with a big coil of rope slung over his shoulder.

'Where are you off to now?' I asked.

'Believe it or not to the prison. I have permission to give lessons on seamanship to the inmates.'

'And what is the rope for?'

'Oh, today's practical lesson is on knots and splices.'

'You had better watch they don't learn about rope ladders, as it won't be the Royal Navy judging you this time,' I teased him. His freckled face lit up in a wide grin.

'All right. No rope ladders, I promise.' Unfortunately, there are not many people like Mike Bailes left in this fast moving world of ours.

*   *   *

Shortly after speaking to Mike in Port Vila, I met the Bulgarian couple Julie and Doncho Papazov, who had successfully crossed both the Atlantic and the Pacific oceans in a ship's lifeboat. When the Papazovs made their landfall from Gibraltar on the coast of Cuba, they were immediately arrested as spies. No one would believe that they had sailed all that distance in such a small boat, and when, on their insistence, the Cubans phoned the Bulgarian embassy in Havana the reaction was the same.

'What two Bulgarians in a sailing boat? Impossible. Of course they are spies, comrade, so just keep them locked up.' Eventually phone calls back home got their voyage confirmed and they were let out of jail, but they still regret their decision to make for Cuba in the naive hope that a fellow Communist country would give them a friendlier reception. Later on I met the Papazovs in Bulgaria, where they had just completed a circumnavigation on their 45 ft ketch *Tivia*.

Aslan's *Experiment*

Few people can have left home on a cruise as green and inexperienced as Beverly and Scott Wilmoth. The idea to go cruising was just an impulse. One

Julie and Doncho Papazov learned about long distance sailing on converted lifeboats. Later with daughter Yana on their 45 ft ketch *Tivia*, they became the first Bulgarians to sail around the world.

summer Sunday some friends had taken them for a sail on Lake Ray Hubbard in Texas. Later over drinks they all agreed that sailing around the world would be fun. It certainly sounded more fun than the life Beverly and Scott were leading as garage owners in Texas. Without giving it much more thought, they decided to embark on a world cruise. 'I've always been impulsive,' smiled Beverly.

A few months later they bought a 27 ft sailing boat, to learn a bit about sailing, although it took them several months to realise that they had rigged it the wrong way. Texas was definitely not sailing country, so they set off for California to look for another boat. They were so taken by the second boat they saw, *Aslan*, a 41 ft Kettenburg fibreglass sloop, that they immediately bought her. From then on, events began to snowball and only one year after their first Sunday afternoon sail, they had already set a date for departure. In the turmoil of leasing Scott's business, selling their house and other preparations, they had had little time to learn about boat handling, seamanship or such practical matters as navigation. They left San Diego in 1977 for the two thousand mile trip to Hawaii as almost complete innocents.

The only chart for the area which they had on board showed Hawaii as a speck in the corner. In the rush before leaving, Scott had found a young Australian yachtsman in San Diego harbour, who showed him how to use the sextant and work out a sight. After six days on the ocean, Scott decided to have a go at his first sight. At noon he managed to get a reading, but when the pair tried to work out their position, they found they had forgotten completely even which books and tables the Australian had told them to use. For four days they pored over Mary Blewitt's manual of navigation, figuring out how to do the calculations. No wonder then that nineteen days after leaving San Diego, when Hawaii appeared just where it should be, it gave them one of the biggest thrills of their landlubbing lives.

After three months in Hawaii, they sailed on to the Marquesas and across the Pacific to Tahiti, Samoa, Tonga and Fiji, gradually becoming more confident in their navigating skills, with each departure being less chaotic than the one before. It was only when *Aslan* sailed across the dateline on the way to Fiji, that they realised something was amiss. First Beverly, then Scott

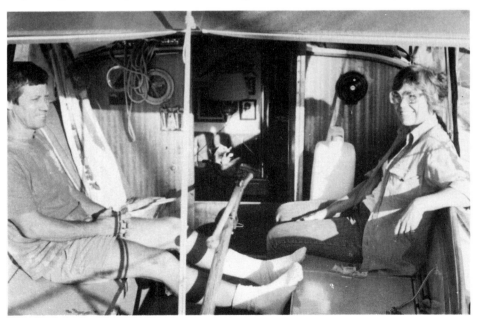

Aslan's crew relaxing in port after a hard sail.

tried to work out their sights, but it did not make sense at all. No one had warned them that west of the 180° meridian, degrees of longitude are counted from west to east, and that sights have to be worked out in a different manner. So it was back to the navigation manual to find the answer. They were lucky to make Fiji, for strong unpredictable currents, unlit reefs and navigational mistakes around the 180° line result in several boats coming to grief in Fijian waters every year.

In their innocence or luck, they had chosen in *Aslan* a well made solid boat with graceful lines, well equipped and able to take them safely across the oceans. Aware of their shortcomings and not being ashamed of their lack of experience, they were always eager and willing to learn from others who were more experienced. After spending six months in New Zealand improving and maintaining *Aslan*, they left for Australia across the notorious Tasman Sea.

'We have never left a port so well prepared,' Beverly told me on the eve of their departure. Although the idea of a world cruise had been in the back of their minds, they had set off for only one year to see if they enjoyed sailing. They found that they loved it.

'We met great people and just sailed farther and farther. By the time we got to New Zealand, it was just as easy to go on around.' After nearly three years of cruising, they sailed via South Africa across the Atlantic to the Gulf of Mexico and Texas, having logged over 30,000 miles on *Aslan*. They were no longer green, but experienced sailors. Aptly, their personal motto is simply

'Learn as you go!'

CHAPTER FIVE

Why Lost? Forty Losses Investigated

The Fastnet disaster of 1979 sent shivers down the spine of every sailor throughout the world. 'Could it happen to me?' was probably the first thought that flashed through everyone's mind, especially in the case of those who were actually on the ocean, cruising in faraway places, away from the magnificent rescue facilites that participants in the Fastnet Race had been able to call upon. We were in the South Pacific at the time, on passage from Tuvalu to Fiji. The stark announcement on the BBC World Service news about the heavy loss of life on the opposite side of the globe prompted me to make an immediate check on all safety features on board *Aventura*.

For the last two years we had been sailing in some of the least frequented areas of the world and I had always been aware that if disaster struck, we had absolutely no chance of calling on outside help and had to solve any crisis alone. We had no radio transmitter on board and were thus totally self-reliant. If the worst came to the worst and we *had* to abandon ship, we had at our disposal both an inflatable liferaft and a hard dinghy, which was lashed on the foredeck from where it could be launched quickly if necessary. The raft container was kept near to the cockpit, so as to be able to be launched in the shortest time possible. Also close to hand was a waterproof plastic box containing emergency rations, first aid kit, fishing gear and all the essential items one would need for survival after emergency abandonment. While taking every possible precaution in case we were forced to abandon ship, my main concern had always been to make the boat herself as seaworthy as possible. As more details emerged about the Fastnet disaster, it became increasingly obvious that if some of those involved had had more confidence in their boats, and ultimately in themselves, many more would have survived.

Unfortunately, sailing boats are lost regularly and not only in such tough ocean races, even if it takes a disaster of this magnitude to attract the attention of a media, often only interested in disaster stories. The Fastnet tragedy prompted me to think about boats that had been lost recently and I was shocked to find that I could list immediately twenty such boats that I knew about personally. Out of the one hundred and fifty boats included in my surveys, at least five have since been lost, while several more have narrowly missed the same fate.

Cruising boats spending the hurricane season at one of the anchorages in Tahiti, a decision that proved disastrous for many during the cyclones of 1983.

Over the last ten years the number of long distance voyages has increased dramatically and probably the increase in boats lost is proportional to this. Yet, compared to earlier small boat voyages, we have at our disposal today better charts, fairly reliable weather information, satellite tracking and warning of tropical depressions and storms, advanced aids to navigation, and improved instruments. Furthermore, present day boats are generally made of stronger materials than those of our predecessors. Taking all these factors into consideration and even allowing for the fact that some of today's voyages are perhaps more ambitious than those of yesteryear, these losses still appear to be disproportionately high.

During the last few years I have gathered material on boats lost and attempted to analyse some of the reasons why. Although the conditions under which these tragedies occurred varied enormously and sometimes precise causes were difficult to ascertain, the main reasons fell into three broad categories, collision, sinking or foundering in open water, and wrecking on reefs or shores. In several cases the causes were interrelated.

Collision with Flotsam

Collision caused the sinking of five of these boats. Two New Zealand boats sailing in the Pacific, *Pono* and *Southern Kiwi*, hit unidentified objects at night and sank quickly. Both crews abandoned ship and were later rescued. Unfortunately, at night it is virtually impossible to avoid such objects, which may include containers lost by ships (those containing a lot of polystyrene packing do not sink and could theoretically float forever), fragments of docks or jetties, navigation buoys adrift, or tree trunks.

Such collisions with unidentified objects, whether by night or by day, are becoming a major hazard for boats on passage and the nature of the object floating just under the surface is seldom identified. Several boats have been lost this way during various transatlantic races, as also was the British yacht *Misty Blue*, on passage from the Canary Islands to the West Indies. The boat struck an underwater obstruction in mid-Atlantic and the damage was so grave that it started sinking rapidly. Peter and Frances Tate, with their three daughters, abandoned the boat for their liferaft, from which they were rescued twelve days later by a Norwegian bulk carrier, after having drifted 400 miles.

Whales

Mysterious collisions have often been blamed in the past on whales, due mainly to their habit of sleeping on the surface oblivious to anything around them, especially a sailing boat making little noise through the water. It was no mystery, however, for two New Zealand boats lost in the South Pacific, who collided with whales in broad daylight. *Snow White*, returning home from a race in Fiji, was bowling along at over seven knots and, although hand-steered and with a full watch on deck, only saw the injured whale *after* the collision. *Dauntless* was at the time on passage from New Caledonia to New Zealand, motoring in calm weather. Three sperm whales, a male, female and calf, were sighted at a safe distance, but the calf made for the boat for a closer look. Probably sensing danger, its mother rammed the boat, holing it amidships. With blood spouting from the injured whale, the bull also joined in the attack, the violent impact lifting the light displacement 50 ft boat out of the water. The crew managed to launch the two liferafts, while skipper Frank Innes-Jones sent out repeated Mayday calls on his portable ham radio, which had been wired up to an emergency battery kept for just such an event. The signal was picked up by an amateur enthusiast in New Zealand, which triggered off a search operation, and the shipwrecked sailors were rescued by a freighter less than 24 hours after losing their boat.

Ironically, we had parted company with *Dauntless* only a few days earlier in Port Vila, when I had been involved in a lengthy but friendly argument with Frank on the merits of using light displacement boats for cruising. I had expressed my worries about the inherent weakness of a lightly built hull, only to be reassured by Frank that *Dauntless* had been equipped with watertight bulkheads fore and aft for this very reason. Unfortunately, not even an experienced skipper like Frank could have foreseen the million-to-one chance of being rammed amidships by an infuriated sperm whale.

This was, incidentally, Frank and Shirley Innes-Jones' second shipwreck. Thirty years earlier, while returning home on the coastal trader *Awahou*, she hit a reef south of Fiji, but was fortunately kept afloat by her cargo of empty oil drums. Five days later they were all saved by an American cruiser.

Although there is still little documented evidence that whales will attack entirely without provocation, collision with a whale either resting or sleeping on the surface may well result in an attack either by the wounded animal itself or by one of its mates.

The trimaran *Spaciety* while on passage to the Marquesas was surrounded by a pod of killer whales, one of whom rammed one float and holed it, although the skipper Larry Pooter was not sure if it was meant as an

Strongly built *Galatea IV* survived a collision at night with a whale in the Bismarck Sea.

aggressive action or was just curiosity. He felt that the whales were not purposively aggressive, as they appeared concerned and stayed with the boat, peering in through the hole at him as he repaired the hull, an action he found quite disconcerting.

Two boats, *Galatea IV* and *Gambol*, collided with whales at night, the former in the Bismarck Sea off New Guinea, the latter in the South Atlantic. Both were sailing at six to seven knots at the time and were fortunate to escape without structural damage. *Galatea IV* arrived in Madang after the collision with all stanchions and the pushpit stove in along one side by the whale's gigantic tail, which passed only a few inches over the head of Marg Miller, who was sitting on watch in the cockpit, too shocked to move. While on passage from South Africa to Brazil, *Gambol* encountered one day a large number of whales, but they all kept away from the boat. During the night however, while running fast before the South Easterly tradewinds, the boat collided with a whale and came to an abrupt halt. A slight leak developed forward, where the fibreglass sheathing had cracked, but subsequent inspection of the hull revealed only slight damage to the sturdily built boat. Like *Galatea*'s skipper, Stuart Clay was also thankful that *Gambol* was strong enough to withstand such an impact.

Collisions with Ships

Being run down or colliding with a ship did not appear to be the cause of any loss among my sample of forty boats, although it could be one of the explanations for at least two boats, which have mysteriously disappeared in the Pacific for unknown reasons. From Slocum to Colas, sailing boats have disappeared at sea without trace, and being run down by a ship is still regarded by many as possibly the greatest danger at sea. The only solution to this is careful watchkeeping.

This was an expensive lesson learned by Denny Moore of *Prospector* when the boat collided with a fishing trawler in heavy weather off the Australian coast. Although *Prospector* was showing lights, no one was actually on deck at the time, as it was the watch changeover period and Denny was below making a cup of tea. The trawler skipper saw *Prospector* only at the last moment and tried to turn away but the trawl doors snagged on *Prospector*'s bowsprit, smashing it and crushing the pulpit. The boat was towed into Sydney, where both skippers were found equally responsible.

Prudence does not always guarantee the safety of a small boat, as both *Ondine* and *Atair II* discovered, both boats being skippered by ex-Navy officers. While transiting the Panama canal and sharing a lock with a large

Classic beauty on the modern *Atair II* whose skipper Klaus Kurz puts his faith in a strong steel hull.

freighter, *Ondine* sustained serious damage to her pulpit and stanchions from her own lines caused by the turbulence created when the freighter started up her engines. More serious damage was caused to *Atair II* and several other yachts, when the Cunard Countess ran aground in Fort de France in February 1982. Trying to come afloat, the Captain ordered full power ahead, creating a huge wash in the small basin. The stern and selfsteering gear of *Atair II* were smashed against the dock by a schooner that had broken its lines, while over twenty yachts were damaged when their mooring lines snapped. The shipping line declined to accept responsibility and the yachts had to finance their own repairs.

Weather

Several boats have been lost recently during tropical revolving storms, which are called cyclones, hurricanes or typhoons depending on the area in which

The wreck of *Desiderade*, one of the many casualties of cyclones Veena and Reva.

they occur. The skippers of these boats took the risk of sailing through a known hurricane area during the hurricane season. The yacht *Drambuoy* left Mauritius bound for South Africa too late in the season, which in the South Indian Ocean extends from November until March and was caught on Christmas Eve by Cyclone Claudette. *Drambuoy* disappeared without trace. A similar fate befell *Crusader* whose skipper also disregarded all warnings and set off across the Bay of Bengal in the midst of the cyclone season and hasn't been heard of since. The fast racing trimaran *Captain Bligh* was lost during the cyclone season in the South Pacific. The skipper had assured me earlier, when I spoke to him in the Solomon Islands about his intended route across the cyclone area, that his boat was so fast he could outrun any tropical depression.

In spite of the number of boats lost every year in the tropics during the summer months, when the incidence of tropical storms can be as high as one per month in certain areas, many skippers disregard the dangers and choose to stay behind. In March 1982 Cyclone Isaac swept through the Tongan archipelago, causing the loss of several boats spending the hurricane season anchored at Neiafu in the Vava'u group. Out of fourteen cruising boats only four escaped with little damage. The situation was repeated several times the following year in French Polynesia, when three cyclones wreaked havoc on islands in the Tuamotus and Tahiti, with a heavy toll of damage and loss of

DIAGRAM 2. *World Distribution of Tropical Storms.*

Area	Jan	Feb	Mar	Apr	May	Jun	Jul	Aug	Sep	Oct	Nov	Dec
Caribbean and Southern USA						■	■	■	■	■		
East North Pacific						■	■	■	■			
West North Pacific						■	■	■	■	■	■	■
North Indian Ocean					■	■	■	■	■	■	■	■
South Indian Ocean	■	■	■								■	■
South West Pacific	■	■	■								■	■

boats. Although this area has a lower incidence of cyclones than elsewhere in the Pacific region, some skippers mistakenly regard it as hurricane proof, in spite of advice to the contrary.

LIGHTNING

Being struck by lightning could be another cause of mysterious disappearances. At least one tropical thunderstorm I have been through was of such incredible violence, that it left no doubt in my mind whatsoever that any of those tremendous bolts of lightning would probably spell the end of us if we were struck. This was between Samoa and Tonga. Another area of violent thunderstorms, especially during the North West monsoon, is the Bismarck Sea. *Rigadoon* was struck by lightning during such a storm off northern New Guinea and, although most of their equipment was earthed, all electrical gear on board was destroyed. Even their cassettes were erased. Fortunately the structure of the boat suffered no damage.

Fittings Failure and Structural Damage

While one can keep out of the hurricane belt during the bad season, some internal faults are more difficult to detect. Although none of the cases in point were known to be lost as a result of internal faults, apart from engine failure which is considered later on, two boats narrowly escaped being lost. A child sleeping under the table raised the alarm on board South African yacht *Seafari*, which was taking part in the Cape to Rio race, when seawater started gushing into the main cabin from a mysterious source. The crew were on the point of abandoning the boat when the skipper fortunately traced the leak to a loose hose clip on the engine seawater intake.

When the French yawl *Calao*, while on passage from Wallis to Fiji in heavy weather, dropped off a wave, the force of the fall split open a seam on the twenty year old wooden boat. Although taking in water heavily, by using all pumps and moving the engine intake hose to draw water from the bilge, *Calao* reached the island of Futuna. With the help of friends from the yacht *Alkinoos*, the crew temporarily patched up the leak.

Other possible internal causes, which could have fatal results, are the destruction of through-hull fittings by electrolysis, and explosion caused by bottled gas or other volatile materials. Corroded seacocks account for the sinking of several boats at their moorings, although I know of no yacht lost as a result of such failure while actually cruising. Nevertheless the danger of a skin fitting or a seacock passing away while at sea is very real, and on *Aventura* I have prepared a selection of wooden plugs which fit every hole in the hull. Each plug has its destination clearly written on its side, and they are kept at an arm's length from the cockpit. In an emergency a plug could be quickly hammered into the failed fitting from the outside. In an equally accessible place a snorkel and a mask are kept ready to grab in an emergency.

An explosion on board can also spell disaster, and such a violent explosion has been suggested as the reason for the disappearance of *Valhalla*, while on passage from American Samoa to Tonga. Some wreckage of the boat, which had a radio transmitter on board, but didn't send out a call for help, was later found washed ashore in Western Samoa.

Wrecking

By far the majority of the boats whose loss I have investigated were wrecked on reefs or shores, or were driven ashore while at anchor in bad weather. The losses can be attributed to a multitude of causes, such as erroneous navigation, poor watchkeeping, over-reliance on the engine, bad planning, running for shelter, anchoring in exposed places or failure of ground tackle.

NAVIGATIONAL ERROR

At least one third of the boats concerned were lost as a direct result of errors of navigation, although these were often compounded by some of the other factors already mentioned.

Six boats were wrecked at night and, because the skippers thought that they were in a safe place, no one was on watch when disaster struck. Several of the skippers admitted afterwards that if someone had been on deck, the reef could have been either sighted or heard in time, and possibly avoided. As three of these were singlehanded (*Tehani III*, *Moana* and *Happy*), a permanent watch was out of the question, although in all three cases the reefs which they struck were several miles off their estimated positions. *Tehani* was lost on a reef in Fiji's Lau Group only minutes after her skipper, Jan Swerts, had gone to his bunk convinced that he was well past a particular reef. Ray Quint lost his *Moana* under similar circumstances in Micronesia, while the singlehanded skipper of *Happy*, on passage from Malaysia to Sri Lanka, missed the latter altogether and ended up on a reef in the Maldive Islands, nearly 400 miles further west.

The only conclusion I can draw from some of these wreckings is that a haphazard approach to watchkeeping has been brought about by many skippers relying completely on selfsteering. As far as I know all nine boats wrecked on reefs were on selfsteering when lost. Similarly, it appears that people rely on their engines to get them out of trouble. The loss of *Grockle*, at Penrhyn in the Northern Cook Islands, most probably could have been avoided if a flat battery had not failed to start her engine, when the boat was being driven onto the nearby reef by swell and current. *Tio Pepe*, after having been sailed successfully by a delivery crew from England halfway around the world to Fiji, was wrecked one hundred miles from her destination for exactly the same reason, an engine which failed to start promptly. The loss of a French boat on the windward reef at Wallis, also in the South Pacific, was equally traumatic as the boat had been totally becalmed for several hours and the hapless crew could only watch helplessly as the boat was eventually driven onto the reef by the swell and destroyed. Again, it was a non-starting engine that got the blame.

Unfortunately it is generally impossible to anchor on the ocean side of a coral barrier reef as the coral rises almost vertically from the ocean bottom. Depending on the size of the boat and the availability of a sufficiently powerful and reliable outboard engine, some people have managed to tow themselves out of danger with their dinghy, while on engineless *Jellicle*, a large sweep has been used to get the 25 foot Folkboat out of a dangerous area when there was no wind.

Navigational error or the inability to assess the actual position correctly resulted in the loss of three of the more remarkable boats featured in my surveys. The elegant *Orplid*, formerly the *Hamburg VI*, a training ship for

German Navy cadets, was lost inside the Great Barrier Reef of Australia. Sailing along in daylight in the vicinity of Cooktown, the skipper failed to identify a submerged reef poorly marked on the chart. The boat struck the reef and was so badly damaged under the waterline that it could not be salvaged. It was a tragic loss for Rolf and Stefani Stukenberg, who decided to follow the Viking custom and set the wreck alight.

The fifty-year-old schooner *Hawk*, previously known as the *Seven Seas*, and sailed by Errol Flynn and President F.D.Roosevelt, was lost under similar circumstances in the Red Sea. After three days of severe storms with poor visibility, so that he was unable to take any sights, skipper Dudley Dewey could only guess at the boat's position. In the early hours of the morning of 26th March 1982, *Hawk* struck the submerged reef fringing St John's Island on the Egyptian side of the Red Sea. The heavy swell pushed the boat firmly onto the reef, the waves washing over the hull. Dudley and Barbara Dewey stayed on board until daylight, then tried to launch their rigid tender, but the half inch dacron line parted in the heavy swell and the dinghy was swept away. Finally they managed to make their way to a rocky ledge half a mile away with their rubber dinghy and outboard engine. After setting up camp, Dudley swam back to the boat and managed to raise the alarm by contacting the yacht *Yaniska* by amateur radio. Eventually the Egyptian air force sent out a helicopter and saved the crew, but the noble *Hawk* had to be abandoned.

The French boat *Drac II* was lost while attempting to enter Parengarenga harbour at the tip of New Zealand's North Island. Because of some difficulty in seeing the leading marks, the skipper took a wrong turn and the strong current quickly grounded the boat. The heavy swell running into the harbour made it impossible to salvage the yacht. It was a simple mistake, but with disastrous consequences for Robert Fabre, a very experienced sailor with one circumnavigation and over 100,000 miles of ocean cruising behind him.

In two of the areas where some of these boats were lost, Fiji and the Red Sea, strong unpredictable currents make navigation extremely difficult at all times, even more so when no sights can be taken because of the overcast skies. Several skippers of the boats lost in these areas complained to me about the frustration of not being able to take a sight for several days and being forced to estimate their position without sufficient reliable information at hand. I could well sympathise with them, as on one occasion, while on passage from Tonga to Fiji, I was unable to take any sights at all for three days and crossed this reef infested area relying solely on my eyes and ears.

The great advantage of SatNav in such a situation is undeniable and several skippers gave me details of potential disasters which had been averted thanks to satellite navigation. The skippers of *Acheta* and *Jenelle* were both convinced that they might have lost their boats in the Tuamotu Archipelago if they had not been able to pinpoint their exact position with the help of their SatNavs. Mac Macauley of *Acheta* had been forced to abandon the plan of entering a lagoon because of the strong current and was trying to leave the area as soon as possible. No sights were possible because of the overcast sky, but his SatNav allowed him to fix the position accurately and avoid all dangers. Also among the atolls of the Tuamotus, William Smith of *Jenelle* plotted his position with a sextant sight shortly before dusk. He set a safe course for the night allowing for a 2½ knot current, only to find on the next satellite passage that the current was in fact running at more like 5 knots and that the boat was within six miles of a reef. Had he relied on astro-navigation alone, the skipper was certain that he would have struck that reef during the night and lost his boat.

AT ANCHOR

Striking a reef at night in a dangerous area, which may be difficult or even impossible to avoid passing through, could be described as bad luck. Losing one's boat while at anchor is, on the other hand, an entirely different matter. Two boats, one at Easter Island, the other at Pitcairn, were driven ashore and destroyed while their crews were visiting the islands. The anchorages at both these islands are known to be unreliable, yet the boats were left unattended for long periods during squally weather. The mast of the wrecked Japanese boat now serves as a flagpole at Hangaroa village on Easter Island, a grim reminder to any sailor venturing that far off the beaten track, never to lose sight of his boat, while visiting the mysterious stone giants. A ferrocement boat from California was the victim of bad weather on Pitcairn, and the inhabitants of this remote island still recall bitterly how they stood by helplessly as the boat pounded on the rocks in the same spot where their mutinous ancestors had burnt and scuttled their *Bounty*. They were upset because they had repeatedly warned the skipper to return to his boat in the deteriorating weather. A third boat was lost at Niue, another island in the South Pacific, while her crew were visiting ashore. The boat had been left on a mooring laid down for visiting boats, but during an unexpected onshore squall the mooring cable parted and the boat was blown onto the rocks.

Anchoring in exposed places is a risk that is sometimes difficult to avoid if one wishes to visit less frequented places. The Australian boat *Korong II* was nearly lost in such an anchorage in the Ha'apai group of Tonga, when it was driven onto the nearby reef by a strong squall during the night. The boat had been anchored so close inshore, that before the engine could even be started, she hit the reef, damaging the propeller blades and jamming the rudder. Unable to steer or move, the boat was driven onto the reef from where it was

Aventura at anchor in Bounty Bay, the exposed anchorage on Pitcairn island, where one always has to be ready to put to sea at short notice if the weather changes.

towed off the next day by a local coaster. Fortunately, being a well built boat, the fibreglass hull survived twelve hours of pounding and came off with no structural damage. In the Pacific, squalls like the one which *Korong II* experienced can sometimes occur *contrary to the prevailing winds*, even during the hurricane-free trade wind season. This should certainly be borne in mind when choosing an anchorage.

Vahine Rii was another boat grounded, whose skipper Tony Pearse felt that it would have been lost if not for its strong steel hull. While at anchor off Palmerston in the Cook Islands, the wind shifted unexpectedly during the night putting the boat on a lee shore. The skipper spent the night hove to under sail, but fell asleep when it got light and woke up to find the boat aground on the reef. Eventually he managed to come off with the help of the engine. This was a course of action denied to *Madame Bertrand*, when it was driven onto a reef after its anchor chain broke in Tubuai, in the Austral Islands. The engineless boat was eventually pulled off by using a stern anchor and 900 ft of line led to a powerful winch. Similarly, a shift of wind caused *Cornelia* to drag her anchor and run aground in Long Island Sound. The heavy swell smashed the rudder and corrugated the keel, but being a heavily constructed steel boat it survived this treatment and was eventually towed off.

Not of steel but solid teak, *Vanessa* had the most sensational escape after being caught by cyclone Orama while at anchor at Rangiroa, the largest lagoon in the Tuamotu archipelago. The violent swell whipped up by the 100 knot wind caused the anchor chain to snap. *Vanessa* was projected over the fringing reef and driven eight hundred feet onto the island beyond, breaking several coconut trees on the way. The cyclone had increased the level of the water in the lagoon and the entire island was covered with four feet of water. Amazingly little damage was done to the strongly built hull, which was later dragged over logs back to the water with the help of several crews from the Tahiti Yacht Club, who sailed out to Rangiroa especially to help a fellow sailor in distress.

Hardly recovered and back in Tahiti, *Vanessa* was caught by both cyclones Reva and Veena, as were *Volte*, *Stereden Vor* and *Abuelo III*, three other boats featured in the Pacific survey who had survived hurricanes while at anchor. *Pytheas* also came through unscathed during hurricane Alan in Bequia in the Caribbean, when the 120 knot wind caused the ⅜" chain to stretch so badly that it was rendered useless afterwards. Fortunately the chain held, as it did for *Drac II* during hurricane David in Martinique, when eighty boats were lost or driven ashore. Although *Drac II*'s anchor held, the boat was extensively damaged by other yachts being driven into it by the strong wind.

Not so fortunate were several other boats which were lost while at anchor, their skippers having chosen to remain and cruise in the hurricane belt during the wrong season. *Ocean Rover* and *Chimera* were completely broken up as the eye of cyclone Meli swept over their anchorage off Kandavu, in Southern Fiji. According to *Chimera*'s crew the unshackled fury of the cyclone was so violent that amidst the turmoil they did not even realise that their boat had been dismasted. In the calm eye of the storm they managed to swim ashore, together with *Ocean Rover*'s skipper. Two crew members of *Ocean Rover* were drowned and when the storm passed over, nothing was left of the two boats except some floating debris. The trimaran *Zoom* was driven ashore and broke up in Honiara in the Solomon Islands, by a vicious onshore squall, known to occur regularly at that time of year.

Running for shelter in bad or worsening weather has often been regarded as more dangerous than remaining at sea, and the loss of *Maruffa*, described in detail on the following pages, is a case in point.

With more or less justification, most of the skippers who have lost their boats attribute at least part of the loss to sheer bad luck, but none more than the Japanese singlehander Yukio Hasebe of *Pink Mola Mola*. While sailing along the coast of Queensland, in Australia, he fell overboard, although he continued to be attached to the boat by his safety harness. However hard he tried to climb back on board, he could not manage to do it as the boat

Another casualty among the singlehanders, Yukio Hasebe lost his *Pink Mola Mola* off the coast of Queensland.

continued to sail very fast steered by her vane, towing behind her the unfortunate skipper. Yukio could do nothing but watch helplessly as the boat eventually steered herself onto the rocks.

Like Yukio Hasebe, many crews, although losing their boats, had the fortune to be rescued, even if this included some harrowing experiences, like being stranded for several days on a reef or drifting helplessly in a liferaft. Nevertheless lives were lost among the boats that made up this sample, including the complete crews of four boats, three of which left no trace or wreckage.

Reducing the Risks

The main reason for examining carefully the various causes for the loss of a number of boats in the foregoing pages was not so much curiosity, but primarily the wish to single out those dangers which could be avoided. The majority of the losses that came under my scrutiny might have been avoided, and this should be a great encouragement to all those who put to sea in small boats. What then can one do to increase one's safety?

Collisions at night with unlit objects, often low in the water, are practically impossible to avoid, unless one is prepared to stop altogether and heave to, an unacceptable position for any cruising boat. Nevertheless, risks can be minimised by reducing speed at night in areas known to be littered with floating debris or frequented by whales. Without doubt a strongly built hull can greatly reduce the risk of sinking if such a collision cannot be avoided, as in the case of *Galatea IV* and *Gambol*, both of whom collided with whales at night while sailing at full speed. Shortly after hearing of *Galatea*'s encounter with a whale in the Bismarck Sea, we sailed through the same area on *Aventura*. Throughout the day we kept a good lookout for whales or floating trees, while every night at sunset I shortened sail to reduce speed to about four knots, a speed at which I feel a well built boat should be able to survive such a collision without sustaining major damage. Several times during those nights we heard a dull thud as we bumped into tree trunks and other debris washed out to sea by the heavy monsoon rains. One year later, while on passage from Malaysia to Sri Lanka, my daughter Doina asked one evening why we didn't slow down at night any more.

'No need to do it here,' I replied confidently, 'as there are neither floating trees nor whales in this part of the Indian Ocean.'

That very night at 01.00, during Gwenda's watch, I was thrown out of my bunk as the boat hit something hard. We were doing six knots at the time, running under poled out twin jibs, yet the collision was so violent that *Aventura* came to a complete standstill. I ran on deck with a light and saw a massive tree trunk slowly roll up from under our keel. The menacing black shape, with stumps sticking out where thick branches had broken off, disappeared behind the stern as *Aventura* slowly picked up speed in the twenty knot wind. To my great relief the bilge appeared to be dry when I checked it, but a later underwater inspection in port revealed more damage to the hull than I had expected, the hull having been badly scored by the trunk along the entire forefoot. I have no doubt that we were only saved by the strength of our hull and I am equally convinced that some boats I know would probably have been sunk by such a collision.

The very next day in broad daylight, sailing along at full speed in some of the most glorious weather we have ever encountered, we saw a large whale right in front of us sleeping on the surface. Its gigantic back showing only inches above the water and, as we hastily altered course to avoid it by a few feet, it opened one eye and cast us a nasty glance, probably cursing us for having disturbed its siesta.

'No tree trunks or whales around here Dad?' asked Doina with a cheeky smile on her face. It was a lesson I am never likely to forget.

Keeping a good lookout at all times can undoubtedly play a major part in reducing one's risk. Even if a navigational mistake has been made or if overcast weather prevents the taking of accurate sights, a good pair of eyes can still avoid disaster. Sailing at night on dead reckoning along the coast of Papua New Guinea, the New Zealand boat *Maamari* just had time to go about to avoid a reef, which was heard and later seen by the crew on watch. The navigator had laid a course fairly close to the reef, relying on seeing a light before altering course. In fact the light had been out of action for some time, and this example shows how good watchkeeping can avoid disaster.

Even the best and most up-to-date instruments do not make a lookout obsolete, and the fact that modern ships equipped with the entire range of navigational instruments are still wrecked proves this point. Generally reefs do not show up well on small radar screens, yet I found that reefs on the windward side of islands always break, except in the calmest of weathers, and are thus audible and visible even at night. Even on the lee side, reefs are often visible, especially when there is some swell. Of the twelve boats in this sample, which were lost on reefs, six were wrecked during the day and it is a matter of speculation if the remaining six could have taken avoiding action in time. Two of these skippers, both singlehanders, admitted that the reefs could have been either heard or seen, had they been awake at the time.

In extremely bad weather, however, the sighting of reefs can be almost impossible. Unable to make the entry into the lagoon at Wallis before dark, I remember one unpleasant night hove-to above 25 miles off the reef. Torrential rain and flying spray in the forty knot wind made me realise it would be impossible to distinguish a reef until almost on top of it. Under such conditions one must be exaggeratedly prudent.

The avoidance of collision in good light should be possible by all those prepared to keep a permanent lookout, so that avoiding action can be taken before it is too late. The days when power gave way to sail without question are fast disappearing and, with an ever increasing number of ships being reluctant to alter course to avoid a small sailing boat in their path, it is safer to assume that a ship on a converging course is not going to give way and to take whatever action is necessary in good time.

On several occasions, both in broad daylight and at night, we have been forced to take avoiding action as the ships in question did not appear to be aware of our presence and most certainly showed no intention of altering course. This is something that has also happened to many of the skippers I spoke to. Once, having to use my engine to get out of the way of a small freighter in bad weather in the Black Sea, a wave lifted *Aventura* up level with its bridge. From 100 feet away I looked straight through the bridge. It was completely deserted with no one at all on watch.

There is no real excuse for neglecting one's watches *even when off known shipping lanes*, as the most deserted areas of the ocean can be crossed by fishing boats, naval ships, research vessels, submarines and, of course, other yachts. In one particular incident, two cruising yachts did collide at night off Tonga, fortunately gently and without much damage. Both skippers were convinced that the area was so deserted that it wasn't necessary to have anyone on watch, nor were they showing any lights. When the skippers had got over the shock of this mild collision, they at least had the pleasure of realising that they were friends and hadn't bumped into each other since leaving California.

Careful and accurate navigation should be the prerequisite for any cruising boat, yet almost one third of the boats in question were wrecked as a direct result of gross navigational errors. During my previous surveys I had the chance to discuss the subject of navigation with over one hundred skippers and I was surprised in several cases at the lackadaisical approach to navigation in general, especially to astro-navigation. Many skippers appeared to rely too heavily on dead reckoning and failed to update their positions regularly, with the result that if and when the weather did close in, their positions were inaccurate and badly out of date. Besides keeping a carefully updated position, many of these boats would not have got into trouble if their skippers had decided to heave to, either to wait for daylight, for better weather or, at least, for a clear sky to take a reliable sight.

Many skippers, however, like myself, prefer to take as many sextant sights as possible, allowing a continual update of position. After having lost half a dozen towed log impellers to hungry fish, who nonetheless ignore the tastefully decorated lures trailing behind *Aventura*, I have stopped using the log in areas where the rate and direction of current are known to be unreliable. My guestimates, based on the latest sights, have become increasingly accurate, although I still prefer to stop and heave to the moment I start having doubts about our actual position. As darkness usually lasts twelve hours in the tropics, we have sometimes hove to as far as thirty miles from our intended objective. Such a wide safety margin would have taken care of any current up to $2\frac{1}{2}$ knots and still allowed us to reach our destination by noon the following day, if we started sailing again as soon as it got light.

The Lau or Eastern Group of Fiji is one of the most dangerous areas in the world; several cruising boats have come to grief in these reef strewn waters every year. Although the charts are fairly accurate, only a few dangers are marked by lights and the distances are too great to allow the prudent navigator to pass all dangers in daylight. Currents in the area are strong and unpredictable. To make things even more difficult than they are already, most boats arrive in this reef area after a 200 mile passage from Tonga. Although well to the east of the 180° meridian, Tonga has decided to keep the same date as her nearest neighbour to the west, Fiji. As a result, local time in

Tonga is GMT +13; rather than GMT −11, as it should be. This also means that the official day in Tonga is one day ahead of her GMT day. Most boats arrive in Tonga from the east, unaware that in fact in Tonga today means tomorrow. After their first visit ashore, all crews change their time and date to the local standard and often do not give the matter another thought. The real problem starts on the next leg of the voyage, to Fiji, when many navigators forget to set back their time by 24 hours. Working out a sight by using the wrong day entry in the Nautical Almanac can result in latitude errors of up to twelve miles, with possible fatal consequences in an area where some passes are only a few miles wide.

Poor watchkeeping, over-reliance on selfsteering devices, and gross errors in navigation are interrelated factors which together have caused the loss of at least ten of the boats examined. Obviously, the problem was compounded by the fact that several of these were singlehanded. Yet even singlehanders can try and keep out of trouble by following the example of old salt Albert Steele of *Peregrine*, who often prefers to heave to and rest in daylight, thus giving other ships a chance to see him. It also allows him to be alert at night or before passing through a dangerous area.

The observance of certain old rules of good seamanship would have also saved some of these boats, such as choosing one's anchorage carefully, possibly using two anchors in exposed places, checking out the reliability of a mooring cable, or by just leaving a bad anchorage and putting to sea before it was too late. While at Honiara, in the Solomon Islands, at the start of the cyclone season when strong onshore squalls could be expected nearly every day in the exposed anchorage, I became a joke among the other skippers when I religiously left the anchorage and hove to well offshore as soon as a squall approached. Once a freighter broke her moorings, and drifted onto the other boats; another time the winds were so strong that most boats dragged their anchor, yet none of the other skippers left with me and all seemed contented to ride out the squalls at anchor. Yet only a few days after our departure, both the trimaran *Zoom* and a local boat were completely broken up during exactly one of those violent onshore squalls.

Many boats are lost throughout the world for the simple reason that they are in the wrong place at the wrong time of year, yet this is a danger which should be the easiest to avoid. The hurricane or cyclone seasons are well known and sufficient data about tropical storms is now available to allow the prudent navigator to choose a relatively safe area for cruising. Some people, however, still choose to face the risk and continue cruising during the bad season in areas subjected to tropical storms. After the loss of *Ocean Rover* and *Chimera* during cyclone Meli, nearly every skipper I spoke to the following year was heading out of the area, bound for New Zealand, Australia or Papua

New Guinea. Even so, being on the edge of the season myself and worried about it, when I asked the skipper of *Pretender* where he was heading for the hurricane season, I was amazed to receive the reply, 'What hurricane season?' Fortunately, such innocence is rare.

Among all those boats which were wrecked under a variety of circumstances, only a handful could be attributed to unavoidable causes. *Pono*, *Southern Kiwi* and *Misty Blue* were sunk after colliding with unidentified objects, *Ponsonby Express* and *Valhalla* vanished at sea when no extreme weather conditions had been reported and their disappearance may never be explained; while the loss of *Pink Mola Mola* could be ascribed to bad luck and nothing else. Luck, whether good or bad, can still play a major part in the safety of our boats. Not for nothing did Willie Willis, the singlehanded raft navigator, maintain that everyone who sets off across the oceans needed an angel on each shoulder. If, besides such heavenly support, one does not leave all watchkeeping to those angels, at the same time paying attention to the accuracy of one's navigation, boat losses could be reduced to a minimum. Unfortunately some of the examples cited seem to point to a low standard of seamanship, but this is a human factor that can be remedied. However, for those who are prepared to approach the sea with prudence and the respect it deserves, and this includes a great deal of serious preparation, a world cruise has every chance of being completed successfully.

THE LOSS OF *MARUFFA*

No one stepping on board *Maruffa* could fail to notice the happy atmosphere among her crew, eight young people always cheerful and full of the joy of living. During a year of cruising together they had cemented their friendships and evolved a tangible communal life. Sitting around the large table in *Maruffa*'s spacious cabin, some of the crew related with relish their adventures sailing *Maruffa* across the Pacific. A quiet young American girl sitting in one corner added a few words and at first I was surprised to find that she was *Maruffa*'s owner, the person who had brought everyone together and created around her such an exceptional atmosphere.

Kit Greene had cruised the Pacific before as crew, so when she inherited a considerable sum of money, she knew exactly what she wanted to do. A student of astrology, even the stars at the moment of her inheritance told of a maiden waiting for a sailing boat. Kit was planning to set off with a group of friends on a voyage around the world and now they only needed the boat. She found a Captain in Steve Sewall and together they toured New England looking for her dream boat. It took a long while, but eventually in Maine they

There was always a happy atmosphere on board *Maruffa* among the young crew who sailed her across the Pacific.

discovered *Maruffa*. She was one of Philip Rhodes' classic yachts built in Maine in 1935. She was a 63 ft yawl built of mahogany on oak frames but badly neglected and in need of attention. Designed as an ocean racer and cruiser, she had a fine history behind her as a private yacht cruising the oceans of the world, from the Mediterranean to the Pacific. Later, under Kit Greene's ownership, she had been used as a whale research vessel in the North Atlantic by the Woods Hole Oceanographic Institute. In 1976 *Maruffa* took part in the Tall Ships race from Bermuda to Newport and was with the fleet in New York on the 4th July for the 200th anniversary of American Independence.

Maruffa was just waiting for someone like Kit to restore her lovingly to her former glory, while astrology gave Kit the symbol of a winged triangle for her dream boat. By the time *Maruffa* was completely refitted and ready to sail, Kit's friends had gone ahead with other plans, so she had to set about finding a new crew. It wasn't too difficult in New England to find likeable young people, who were game for a world cruise aboard a beautiful sailing boat with all living expenses paid for.

One of Kit's long term plans was to sail to Egypt, led by her star, to pursue her interest in studying ancient astrology. *Maruffa* was even an Arabic name, meaning *The Swift One*. First however she sailed down to the Caribbean, through the Panama Canal and to the Galapagos, where the young crew spent

Maruffa sailing off the New Zealand coast shortly before being wrecked.

carefree days swimming and diving among the seals and observing the unique wild life on the islands.

Sailing across the Pacific some of the crew changed here and there, but the atmosphere remained the same, with Kit generating a quiet serenity around her. In New Zealand, Kit and her seven friends worked hard for several weeks giving *Maruffa* a major refit; everything was checked and serviced. A new boom and rudder were fitted, wood was scraped, sanded, repainted and revarnished, the eight of them working a daily twelve hour stint. In tip-top condition *Maruffa* then showed her paces in the annual Tall Ships race in the Bay of Islands, before setting off to sail around the southern tip of New Zealand, into Fiordland, and across the Tasman Sea to Australia.

New Zealand's South Island is renowned for its wild weather and lack of shelter, and sailing with a reduced crew of six, *Maruffa* met stormy conditions rounding into the Foveaux Straits. A backstay parted and they decided to run for shelter. Tragedy was poised to strike. Entering a small bay at night, relying on the depth-sounder and radar to grope their way in, they clipped a projecting ledge and the huge seas soon pushed *Maruffa* onto the rocks. It was a black night. In the rough conditions they had difficulty launching the liferafts to get ashore. Trying to rescue one of the liferafts that had been washed overboard, Alex Logan got caught between the side of the boat and the rocks and, in moments, the pounding boat severed his leg through completely at the thigh. Another crewman quickly made a tourniquet from his belt and the freezing water helped to staunch the flow of blood. They managed to get ashore with one liferaft and only then did one of the girls realise that she had lost her thumb. Unable to raise anyone on the radio, the crew spent an anxious night huddled on the cliffs inside the liferaft, trying to keep Alex warm and alive. Only when dawn rose could Steve Sewall trek the few miles to the nearest house to raise the alarm, and soon a helicopter had Alex safely in hospital.

Maruffa meanwhile pounded on the rocks, a giant hole in her side. It was impossible to organise a salvage in that remote part of the world, and the sad end for a classic yacht, with forty years of sailing behind her, came quickly.

The Pacific claims many victims every year, and some dreams must end in tragedy. Yet in retrospect Kit feels that the wrecking of *Maruffa* was one of the most crucial experiences of her life.

'It was very much "us" that night, the group rather than the individual, and our emotions were so tangible, as if they had an existence outside as well as inside each of us. I think of other people's tragedies now with a new awareness, and can identify with what they feel. We are all thankful to be alive.'

Out of tragedy came understanding, and Kit Greene still includes sailing among her future plans.

ALBERT STEELE

I almost missed *Peregrine* tucked away in a corner of Nuku'alofa's small port. Battered and stained, the 40-year old cutter did not look all that different from the local boats surrounding it. My eye was caught though, as her white haired owner Albert Steele stepped jauntily ashore, with his Tongan lady Malia on his arm. He wore his 63 years lightly, his tanned and furrowed face pierced by bright blue eyes. After exchanging a few words, it was clear that here was an exceptional man of the sea. Over several evenings of talk on board *Aventura*, I learned of his lifetime of seafaring adventure and the salty wisdom he had to offer.

Albert had always loved the sea. As a child he used to climb a water tower near his home to watch the square riggers sailing up the Delaware river. He was only twelve years old when he ran away from home and joined a small Bermudan sloop, that dredged for crabs in Chesapeake Bay. The sloop's skipper taught the youngster the art of sailing and even now Albert prefers to steer by points, as he learned that first summer.

Although he returned home in the winter, the saltwater coursing in his veins couldn't be long ignored. The remainder of his teenage years were spent as a deckhand on a variety of sailing boats, seiners fishing off Florida and Texas, coasters trading down the East Coast as far as Maine, and open decked sloops transporting cattle from Puerto Rico to the Virgin Islands. He jumped ship, he stowed away, and rarely hit the same port twice. Vividly he recalls the time he was in Cuba when Batista came to power.

'We were forbidden to leave ship, so of course that was the first thing we did. We found a bar, commandeered all the girls, threw out the locals, locked the door and got steadily drunk on monkey rum, while the guns of the civil war boomed out over Havana.'

He went everywhere, did everything, satisfied every whim. He even served six months on an adult chain gang, though still a juvenile, for stealing a bar of soap.

'It did my physique a lot of good,' he laughed. 'I guess I was a bit of a wild kid in those days.'

After a waterside brawl put twenty stitches in his head, he decided to jump ship in Hawaii. For the next two years he sailed to various Pacific islands on the *Islander*, which had been converted to a fishing boat after its famous ethnological expedition to the islands of Polynesia. In Hawaii he also found time to qualify as a hard hat diver and get his 500-ton master's ticket. He had just turned twenty-one.

Hawaii at this time was beginning to get too 'touristy' for Albert and, undaunted by a seaman's strike which prevented him signing on, he just stowed away on a Navy ship to get himself back to the mainland. He tried working ashore as a rigger for a road show touring California, but the lure of the sea was too strong, so he wound up as first mate on a schooner, fishing the Banks of Campeche in the Gulf of Mexico.

In the late 1930s these snapper schooners were the last stronghold of boats working under sail. All the old salts from the square riggers and sailors from the Grand Banks fleet, had gravitated to that corner of the globe. Aged just 23 Albert got his first command and skippered a crew, the youngest of whom was more than twice his age. They were of all nationalities, but all master seamen, who must have sensed the doom of their trade, for every time they put into port they got hopelessly drunk. Albert rigged his 60 ft schooner so he could manage her singlehanded under jib and staysail. Loading his drunken crew, he would sail her out to the middle of the bay, drop anchor and wait for them to sober up before they could set sail for the fishing banks.

World War Two sounded the death knell for large scale fishing under sail. Albert, like so many others, was swept up in the great war machine and found himself transported to North Africa and Italy, first as a rigger in a tank recovery unit and then as a salvage diver. After his discharge he returned to Florida, but the sailing schooners had disappeared. Not daunted, he joined the sponge fishing fleet as a diver working off the coast of Florida. The prices for sponges were high and he earned a good $15,000 a year walking on the sea bed. In 1947 sponges from Greece, which had grown untouched during the war years, started flooding the US market. The price dropped dramatically from $35 to $4 a pound and Albert left to look for work elsewhere.

The next chapter in the odyssey took Albert to California, where he studied modern navigation methods and was before long skippering a tuna boat out of San Diego. For years he followed the tuna up and down the Central American coast, to the Galapagos and Ecuador. After a particularly bad storm off Baja California, Albert thought to himself that there must be an easier way to earn a living. So he turned his back on the sea, moved ashore and dedicated himself to something which had always fascinated him, art and antiques.

The other side of his life was evident in *Peregrine*'s cluttered cabin. A candle in an antique brass stand threw long shadows over shelves crammed with books on period furniture and art history. The bulkheads were hung with old Dutch prints and ancient chronometers. The chart table contained valuable early charts as well as their modern counterparts. It was all that remained of his fine collection of antiques.

During his years ashore, Albert built up a reputation as a specialist in English period furniture. For ten years he refused to even go near the waterfront, but the sea eventually proved the stronger and he satisfied his calling by working part time as a tugmaster.

'I guess I must be the only guy who has given a lecture on 17th century English furniture to a hall full of academics and then ran backstage, put on my overalls and within the hour docked a ship in San Diego harbour. It was an ego trip for me, especially as I never made it past 8th grade at school.' Albert gave one of his infectious chuckles. 'I never had much education, but I've always had a taste for champagne.'

It was a lovely life, he had plenty of money, and had built up a private collection worth a quarter of a million dollars. But on the eve of his sixtieth birthday, Albert took a long look at himself and felt life running like sand through his fingers. The saltwater in his veins gave him the answer. He sold a painting and started looking for a boat.

Never a yachtsman, but always a sailor, he had little use for the sleek modern vessels. It took him a long time to find *Peregrine*, a little ship resembling the ones he had sailed in his youth. She matched Albert perfectly; a classic cutter built almost fifty years ago for the Fastnet race of 1936. Built of pitchpine on oak frames, her seven foot bowsprit gives her an overall length of 45 ft. Above and below decks she is simple and functional. The first thing Albert did was to throw out her engine, which he hated with a 'purple passion', then he loaded her up with the remnants of his art collection, now seriously depleted by two divorces, and set forth.

In 1976 he left California bound for Cape Horn and then the Greek Isles. However Albert did not stick to plans. Nor was he a solitary man and had not planned on being a singlehander, it just turned out that way.

At the end of a lifelong involvement with the sea, Albert Steele in the cosy cabin of ageing *Peregrine*.

'I'm just too careful and after my enthusiastic crew had lost a couple of winch handles overboard, I decided to go it alone.' Not only careful, Albert was cautious, tempered by years of experience and knew how to conserve his energy. As a singlehander he often chose to heave to and rest in broad daylight and good weather, when there was a good chance of his boat being seen by passing ships. He could then rest and stay awake at night or if the weather deteriorated. He was one of the few people who still used a sea anchor, stopping to rest with his double-ended *Peregrine* lying comfortably to a sea anchor streamed from astern.

A trip around the Horn became less and less appealing and making friends on other boats, Albert turned *Peregrine*'s bows west to join the fleet sailing across the Pacific, hoping to find a trace of the atmosphere he had known there more than four decades previously. Tahiti was not at all what he had in mind, but sailing on westward to Tonga he was delighted to find the Polynesian atmosphere he thought had disappeared forever. He decided to stay. As a ticketed captain he was much in demand to skipper local fishing boats, but his plans were only to refit *Peregrine*, sail a little, fish a little, and enjoy the company of pretty Malia.

I met him again in Fiji, where he had gone to have an engine fitted back into *Peregrine*. Pottering in and out of the Tongan reefs in search of shells for a jewellery firm had changed his mind.

With the engine not yet in commission, I towed *Peregrine* from the boatyard in Suva with my dinghy. It was a pleasure to watch the ease and calmness with which he got his 45 footer under sail, every sheet and move carefully synchronised. The weather was miserable, wet and overcast, so it was no surprise to see *Peregrine* still at anchor the next morning, tucked behind the entrance reef to Suva. Albert was in no hurry and I knew he wouldn't take any risks on his trip back through the dangerous Fijian waters to Tonga. Not only singlehanders, but all of us can learn a lot from Albert Steele, sailor from a bygone era.

During the Pacific survey I learnt the sad news of Albert's death from Hugh Brown, who had sailed with Albert, learning many valuable things from him. Hugh's attitude to the sea and the way he ran *Nightwing* was in the same tradition as his mentor, and I was heartened to see that Albert Steele's spirit lives on among those who knew him. Albert's patience, dry humour and special feeling for the sea are a legacy many of today's sailors would do well to inherit.

CHAPTER SIX
The Seawives Have Their Say

The Seawives Survey

The sea is in many respects still an area of male supremacy, yet in the field of cruising many notable achievements would not have been possible without female participation. In spite of this, the women's opinion is usually neglected or not even asked for, not just by their skippers, but also by designers, builders, clubs and often boating magazines. While interviewing skippers, I noticed how on several occasions the wife was told more or less politely not to interfere, even in situations where her contribution could have been of value.

The anchorage at Kerikeri in New Zealand's Bay of Islands, a popular place to spend the cyclone season.

In all fairness, I should point out that on many other boats the skipper readily consulted his mate on points raised in the survey, while on a couple of boats the skippers were women. After being reproached a few times that my questions seemed to be always directed to the skipper, I was ready to admit that I had nearly committed the same mistake, of passing up blindly the rich source of knowledge and practical experience of the female voyagers.

Out of the total of one hundred boats surveyed on practical aspects of seamanship and long distance cruising, eighty had a seawife on board. I use the term 'seawife' loosely, as the eighty ladies concerned included not only wives, but also girlfriends, mothers and independent women cruising on their own terms. Many of them were experienced sailors in their own right and all of them filled the criteria I had set for the skippers, to have been cruising continuously for at least one year and to have covered a minimum of 5,000 miles away from base. The sample was very representative as it included women of all ages, from early 20s to late 60s, married or single, mothers and grandmothers, divorcees and widows. Their range of occupations and interests were just as wide, farmers and doctors, teachers and nurses, businesswomen and housewives.

Wherever possible I tried to talk to the seawives on their own, but when this was not possible, I firmly asked their skipper not to interfere. In a few cases where the skipper still insisted on butting in, I discreetly ignored him and wrote down the wife's version. Even so, I left the occasional heated argument behind me and was quite happy to get into my dinghy and row away.

Decision to Cruise

For all the 80 seawives who took part in the survey, cruising was a way of life and not just a weekend or holiday pastime. The decision to cut off all ties with a shorebound existence for a life at sea must have been for many of them one of the most radical decisions in their entire life, therefore I asked each of them how much the choice of this way of life had been hers. In 43 cases I was assured that the decision had been mutual, the two partners taking the decision together. In eleven cases the decision had been taken solely by the skipper, the wife only having the stark choice of accepting it or staying behind. On the other hand, for the eleven independent women of their own financial means, the decision to go cruising had been entirely theirs. The remaining women gave various percentages to show their participation in the decision making, ranging from 10 to 40 per cent, indicating that in the last resort it had been the skipper's decision that tipped the balance.

'I was blackmailed into it,' said one wife, 'He said he would only marry me if I came with him on a trip around the world in a small boat. So I came.'

The smile with which she said it and the fact that their voyage was one of the longest among those surveyed probably meant that the initial blackmail had turned into a happy memory. Love rather than blackmail had led some of these women to a life afloat, as in several cases they met their skippers somewhere en route, joining the sizeable proportion of boats crewed by couples of differing nationalities.

Effects on Marriage

The passive role played by some of the wives in the intial decision to go cruising can lead to serious problems later on, putting in jeopardy not just the continuation of the voyage, but even the marriage itself. Beryl Allmark, who had already been cruising for twelve years with her husband Alan on *Telemark* when I spoke to her, pointed out, 'Cruising is something you either like doing or you don't. There are so many broken marriages among those who set off sailing, because in most cases it was the husband's decision to go and the wife followed only reluctantly.'

My questions on marriage touched on a subject that many women felt very strongly about and most of them were ready to discuss in a frank and forthright manner. Living together in the small confines of a boat while undertaking long ocean passages exerts considerable stresses on any relationship. At the end of a three year voyage around the world on *Aslan*, Beverly Wilmoth considered the most valuable suggestion she could make to other voyagers was to make sure they could handle being together for long periods at a time. All seawives stressed the importance of a sound marriage, underlining the fact that it was no good taking a shaky marriage to sea. Kathy Becker of *Jocelyn*, summed it up like this: 'The marriage has to be 100 per cent sound for each partner, otherwise it would fall apart.' This was a point of view reiterated by Irmtraud Klein of *Haubaut*, who stressed, 'One should never start off on such a voyage unless you already get on well with each other ashore.'

Another wife admitted that cruising had been an eye opener and she now realised that she had hardly known her husband before. Spending twenty-four hours a day together obviously had an effect on relationships and another woman observed that life on board is very good at pulling people apart. In a lot of cases, however, the cruising life had brought couples closer together.

Dorine Samuelson gets on with repair work on *Swan II* while keeping an eye on Nicky's school work.

Exactly half of the women interviewed felt more dependent on their partner than they did ashore, only two women saying they had become more independent than previously. Several women pointed out that life at sea was different, in that both partners are dependent on each other and have to work as a team.

'As it is us against the elements, we both depend on each other more,' said Betty Eastman of *Con Tina*, a factor no doubt in the partnership which has turned the Eastmans' planned two-year cruise into a permanent way of life.

The couples who had been cruising for a long time, or who had done a lot of sailing together before their present voyage, certainly seemed to enjoy a particularly harmonious relationship. The first year of a cruise appeared to be the crucial period in which relationships are tested. Several wives gave examples of voyages abandoned and broken marriages that they had witnessed while cruising.

The sea is thus a perfect testing ground for marriage, and Karen Huso of *Potpourri* advised potential cruising wives, 'Do some sailing before setting off, so as to make sure that you really want to do it and also that you can live with your husband 24 hours a day.'

Anne Faubert returning from a shopping trip. On most boats provisioning and looking after the children continues to be a job left to the seawife.

Expectations vs. *Reality*

Although the primary decision to change their life style was not always theirs, only three of the seawives considered that cruising had failed to live up their expectations. In fact, out of 80 seawives, 42 stated that the cruising life was better than they had expected. Twenty-five women found cruising very much as they had imagined, neither better nor worse, whereas a further ten admitted that although cruising had lived up to their expectations, they had some reservations. Several of them stated that some aspects were better than expected, while others were certainly worse.

'I like the ports more than I thought I would, and I hate the sailing more than I thought I would. Sometimes I would prefer to see the world by other means,' as Suzanne Hartley of *Tara II* put it.

I was told on several occasions that the rewards of cruising as a way of life were often very different to what the wife had expected before setting off.

'You never get what you think you'll get,' said Jeannette Delvaux of *Alkinoos*. 'That is what makes cruising so challenging. It's definitely not a tourist brochure life, but this is not to say that cruising is not agreeable.' Several wives admitted that they had hoped for a more glamorous life, mostly because their husbands had always talked only about the dreamlike qualities of life on a sailing boat in the balmy tropics. Instead cruising turned out to be much less glamorous, often downright hard and demanding, although some rewards came from unexpected directions. Linda Balcombe of *Starshine* admitted, 'I had a few disappointments, mainly because some of the ideas of what I thought I'd find in the South Pacific were taken from movies.'

While finding cruising life rewarding in a general way, D'Ann McClain of *Windrose* considered it difficult for an independently minded woman to relinquish most of her freedoms:

'There is less freedom on a boat than one expects. A woman has to be prepared to lose her independence, her autonomy. All the important decisions are taken by the skipper. This can be very frustrating to the wife, because ashore many fundamental decisions are taken by her. The wife often runs the house, but would never run the ship.' As to be expected from a businesswoman, D'Ann knew exactly where she stood and was incensed by the chauvinistic attitudes of many skippers, on whose boats the male played an even more dominating part than on land. This view was shared by Dana Nicholson of *Spray*, who is strongly in favour of more female participation in all sailing matters.

'Above all, women must believe in themselves,' said Dana, 'as the only way of counteracting male chauvinism at sea.' On the other hand it was noticeable, especially among the couples who had been sailing for a really long time together, that all important decisions were taken jointly, often the wife dealing with matters which normally are regarded as the province of the skipper.

As in many cases the decision to take up cruising had been initiated by the husband, it was perhaps not surprising that a high proportion of the seawives told me that they had not been really interested in sailing before the plans for the voyage started taking shape. But once the preparations were past the initial stages, most of these seawives began to look at sailing with more enthusiasm. In a few cases the husbands did not have much sailing experience either, so sailing and navigation were learned together.

Generally the break with shore life, family and friends seems to affect women more deeply than men, so I asked all the seawives how much they missed these things. Just over half stated that indeed they missed their family, particularly on special occasions such as Christmas or Thanksgiving. Most of the women who missed their family were mothers who had never before been separated from their children and grandchildren for long periods of time.

Friends were missed less than family; several times I was told that the absence of old friends was more than compensated by the new friends made both in the places visited and among other cruising people.

I reached virtually the same conclusions when I brought up this subject again in my survey of the 12 circumnavigators. For instance, Mary-Louise Stewart of *Kyeri* considered the toughest part of the entire voyage was leaving her grown up children behind.

Even less missed than the friends back home were the shore comforts, most of which are denied to those who choose to live on a small boat. Forty-four of the seawives stated firmly that they did not miss the conveniences of life ashore at all. Those who missed such comforts did not include any women who were on longer voyages, but were drawn from those who had left home recently and for whom these modern conveniences were still fresh in their memories. One thing mentioned by several wives, both among those who missed and those who did not miss their shore comforts, was the shortage of abundant fresh water, which nearly every woman regarded as a great nuisance. Certainly not missed at all was the hardware of a modern home.

'How could I miss them? I've had them all. When you've had a thirteen room house with all the mod cons that go with it, you're glad to be rid of them!' exclaimed Opal McInness of *Mac's Opal*. Similarly Beverly Wilmoth of *Aslan*, who had been used to a large house with all possible amenities back home in Texas, found she was quite happy to live and work in the constricted

Vicki Holmes was one of the fortunate seawives to have a small washing machine on board *Korong II*.

space of a boat with no labour saving devices at all. She had already decided to lead a more simple and modest life when she returned to shore and I was interested to hear from her that in fact they had bought a much smaller house, when they returned from their three year voyage.

'One must be prepared to do the domestic chores as one would have done fifty years ago, such as washing by hand in a bucket,' said Marika Hantel of *Pytheas*. 'If one is not willing to give up shore comforts, it's better not to go at all.'

It was interesting to note that the longer a woman had been cruising, the simpler her life style became. As Susan Hiscock of *Wanderer IV* remarked, 'You just learn to live without these things.' Doing away with some of the machinery of modern living does not mean that all these women lead spartan lives. Many boats are nowadays equipped with freezer or refrigerator, a few have small washing machines and even a microwave oven is not such a rarity any more.

Division of Labour Aboard

Labour division in navigation, boat handling, cooking, washing and most other activities on board played a major part in my survey. On most boats navigation, especially astro-navigation, continued to be regarded as the prime responsibility of the skipper. Thirty-eight seawives told me that they never did navigation of any sort, while fourteen did very little. Out of the total of eighty, only five wives took care of all the astro-navigation on their boats, the remaining twenty-three participated in some measure, on average doing about half the navigation. Among these latter it was more common for the skipper to take the sight and the wife to do the calculations; in most of these cases I was told that the mate had a better way with figures.

Regarding sailhandling, which included raising, lowering and changing sails, as well as reefing, I was somewhat surprised to find that thirty of the seawives never did any sailhandling at all, a further eighteen did very little and even the proportion of work done by the remaining thirty-two only averaged out at 30 per cent. Only one seawife did all sailhandling herself, admittedly on one of the smaller boats. The size of the boat, and implicitly the size of the sails, was the main inhibiting factor. Muriel Bouteleux of *Calao* even specified that she regarded a 40 ft boat as the limit for the strength of the average woman.

While most women left the best part of the deck work to their male partners, this does not mean that during sailchanging the wives are just looking idly on, but usually do the necessary work from the cockpit, either handling sheets or being at the helm if the selfsteering or autopilot is disengaged. From a purely statistical point of view, the seawives surveyed did practically as much boat handling as their skippers. Asked to rate as a percentage their share at the helm, both steering while underway and moving in and out of port, forty-four wives rated their helmwork as 50 per cent, the remaining thirty-six covered the whole range from 10 to 100 per cent.

As the majority of the crew interviewed were couples, seldom taking on additional crew, they had perfected their teamwork, each knowing exactly what to do in a given situation. This was reflected in the precise answers the seawives were able to give me on questions concerning the general handling of the boat. It was particularly noticeable in the question of anchor handling, that those women who normally spent a higher proportion of time at the helm rarely did any anchor work and vice versa. Overall, thirty-six wives never handled the anchor, the remaining forty-four doing an average 50 per cent of this work. It was generally on the smaller boats that the women did a higher proportion of the anchor handling or on the larger boats equipped with electric windlasses.

Because of the physical difference between the sexes, a precise allocation of tasks makes sense, although a number of skippers are still reluctant to relinquish the helm. On many occasions I have watched boats coming in to either anchor or dock with the skipper shouting instructions from the cockpit to a poor woman struggling with several mooring lines or a heavy anchor. Susan Hiscock of *Wanderer IV* made the same point when discussing the division of work on a shorthanded boat:

'Women should know as much as possible about the boat and sailing, so as to take part in the handling of the boat as much as the husband. All things on the boat should be done jointly, yet often the husbands try and make themselves look superior. Coming into congested ports, for instance, the wife should be at the helm and the man at the lines and fending off. It is only vanity on their behalf. They want to be seen to be in control.'

The rest of the questions on labour division were concerned with the domestic chores of cooking, provisioning, washing dishes and clothes. It was these questions which most frequently caused disagreement between skipper and mate, the bone of contention invariably being the percentage of washing up done by either of them. This was the one area of my survey in which my sums hardly ever added up. As on land, the proportion of these chores done by the females was much greater. Forty-one of the wives interviewed did 100 per cent of the cooking, a further ten rated their contribution as 95 per cent and twenty-five as 75 per cent. In this latter category, the wives cooked main meals, while the skippers prepared breakfast. On four boats the women did virtually no cooking, but in two cases they did all the navigation. The overall percentage of the cooking done by the seawives interviewed averaged out at 82 per cent.

A similar percentage (83 per cent) of laundry work was done by the wives, although compared to cooking a higher number claimed to do 100 per cent of all washing. There was no wife who did no laundry at all, although on one boat husband and wife did their own washing. Even the independent single girls did a greater percentage than their own personal laundry. The men appeared to help out more with the washing of dishes, only one third of the women claiming to do all the washing up. The remaining seawives did between nil and 90 per cent of the washing up, the average being 68 per cent.

Regarding provisioning, both short and long term, this was definitely a female responsibility. On most boats the wife decided alone all provisioning matters, while on fourteen boats the provisioning was decided jointly.

Several women pointed out that the skippers should not necessarily be always blamed for the traditional division of work along male/female lines. Often it was the woman's fault, for accepting to be cast into a domestic role without protesting. It was a point that Cynthia Hathaway of *Spaciety* felt particularly strongly about. 'A woman should be assertive, should learn how to sail, how to handle the boat. It's no good spending all your time in the

Muriel Bouteleux trying to find local vegetables to match her French cooking in Papua New Guinea.

galley, because if the man does everything to do with the boat, he naturally expects the woman to do all the housework, like cooking, washing etc.' Muriel Bouteleux of *Calao* entirely shared that opinion. 'All tasks on a boat, from cooking to navigation, should be divided fairly, yet in cooking, laundry and washing up, the same principles seem to operate at sea as on land.'

In fact, Muriel was one of the several mothers included in this survey, who were accompanied by their children. Especially in those cases where the children were under the age of ten, a lot of the women's time was occupied with the children, which obviously left them less time for playing a more active role in sailing the boat.

Emergency Competence

Although several women did not normally do the sail handling, anchor work or navigation, this did not mean that they did not know how to do these things if necessary. In both the Cruising and Pacific surveys I asked the seawives if they could do certain jobs alone in an emergency situation. In each survey, exactly the same proportion of 38 women out of forty assured me that they could sail the boat singlehanded if they had to. A smaller proportion would be able to navigate safely back to a port if the navigator was incapacitated, although the number of competent seawives in this respect was higher in the second survey. In the Cruising survey only 23 women stated that they would be able to carry out any astro-navigation in an emergency situation, whereas 35 of those in the Pacific survey thought they could navigate back to port. Some of these wives, however, pointed out that they would have to make use of the SatNav in their offshore navigation rather than the sextant.

Also with an emergency situation in mind, I asked the wives if they could do other specific jobs alone if the necessity arose, such as bringing the dinghy back on board, getting the anchor up, putting to sea from an anchorage, carrying out simple repairs on the engine and setting the self-steering or autopilot. Out of eighty women questioned on this aspect in the two surveys, 69 women told me that they could bring up the dinghy on their own, a similar number also being able to cope with the anchor and chain or line. Several women felt that they would have a struggle doing this but that in an emergency they might summon the strength from somewhere. The women who could not raise the anchor all complained it was too heavy. I feel that it would be to every skipper's advantage to make sure that on his boat all essential equipment can be handled by the weakest member of the crew. Similarly, several women said they could not raise their rigid dinghies on board alone, but in an emergency situation would not hesitate to leave it behind. An even higher number were perfectly able to put to sea on their own, although in many cases I was told that it meant getting the boat underway with the help of the engine. Among the women who could leave an anchorage on their own, those who were unable to lift the anchor back on deck unaided said they would simply leave it behind, possibly buoyed.

Even if practically every one of the seawives knew how to turn the ignition key and, provided the engine started, could get the boat moving, the engine itself remained a mystery for most women. Only nineteen wives were confident enough that they could carry out at least some simple repairs on their engine. My test question was to ask them whether they knew how to purge their diesel engine if air had entered the fuel system. Although it is one of the most common reasons why a diesel engine may stop running, fifty-nine women admitted that they could not cope with such a problem. Nevertheless, fifteen women were prepared to tackle the engine in an emergency, while two said they would read the manual and have a go. Another experienced seawife, Maria van Zelderen of *White Pointer*, replied that if the engine was broken, she would concentrate on sailing the boat and not try to repair it, perhaps emulating her neighbour moored alongside in Raiatea, Cristina Plantier of *Madame Bertrand*, for whom this question was irrelevant as she sailed on an engineless boat.

'Women should be able to do everything on a boat including navigation, although that doesn't mean they have to do it regularly,' remarked Janice Pickering of *Northern Chinook*.

Setting the automatic pilot seemed to present less difficulties and twenty-two women whose boats were equipped with autopilots knew how to use them. Four boats had no selfsteering device whatsoever, whereas on the remaining sixty-one boats equipped with wind operated selfsteering gears, fifty-four of the seawives were able to set them, only seven being unable to do so.

Those women who were not capable of doing some or most of these jobs alone were aware of their shortcomings and regretted not having become more proficient at sailing before setting off. In fact, it was mostly these less experienced seawives, who suggested that any women comtemplating a long distance cruise would be well advised to try and learn as much as possible about sailing before setting off, as this would not only make their life easier later on, but would also put them on an equal footing with their male partners.

All my hypothetical questions were easily answered by one seawife, June Macauley of *Acheta*, who had the experience of doing all these things in just such an emergency. She had to sail the boat singlehanded eighty miles back to the Mexican mainland after her husband Mac was laid low with a severe case of hepatitis. Once Mac was safely cured, she was glad to have had this experience, because it had given her confidence in her own abilities. This incident emphasises the advice given to seawives by Pascale Fecamp of *Kalabush*: 'It is a priority for a women to be able to sail the boat alone.'

The possibility of the skipper becoming totally or partially incapacitated while on passage is very real and the reluctance of many skippers to delegate any responsibility to their crew can have grave consequences.

This survey has shown that on several boats not only was the skipper in total command, but also that the precautions taken to cope with certain problems in his absence were often inadequate. There are several examples of the crew being forced to cope on their own after the skipper had been put out of action, one of the most poignant being that of a boat on passage from Hawaii to American Samoa. Several days after leaving Hawaii, the skipper, who was in his sixties, collapsed. Up to that moment he had kept a regular schedule with an amateur radio network, so his wife was able to call up the same frequency and request help. It soon became obvious that she had no idea how to sail or handle the boat, work out a position or even start the engine to charge up the batteries when these started getting flat. Eventually, the US Coastguard was forced to send out a plane to parachute a doctor and navigator in the vicinity of the stricken boat. They gave emergency treatment to the skipper and sailed the boat to the nearest island, from where the patient was airlifted back to Hawaii. The very real danger of this kind of emergency occuring on a boat in mid-ocean came to me forcefully during a passage from Sri Lanka to Aden, when for two days I was knocked out by a severe bout of malaria. Fortunately the crew of *Aventura* managed perfectly on their own, showing me that at least on my own boat the skipper was not indispensable.

The Right Age for Cruising

Seventy women considered their present age to be a good age for this kind of life. The eighty women interviewewd included seventeen in the 20–30 age group, thirty-seven in the 30–40 group, twelve between 40 and 50 years old, while fourteen were over 50. Many women pointed out that any age was right for cruising as long as the person was fit and enjoying this way of life. The only group where opinion was divided was among the over-fifties. Even among those saying that their age was right, some of the older women in their sixties would have preferred to have started earlier. For some of these women the real obstacle to setting off earlier was their children, as they did not like the idea of cruising with children on board.

'It would have been nice to go earlier, but then I had four children and that would have complicated matters, whereas now I feel freer, as I do not have that responsibility,' said Madeleine Fily of *Stereden Vor*. A similar dilemma was voiced by Velda Moore of *Prospector*.

'I wished I had started younger, but on the other hand I wouldn't want to be cruising with young children.' Madeleine had her youngest daughter, 16-year-old Emmanuelle with her, and another nineteen mothers among the eighty seawives were sailing with their children. Although most were quite contented to cruise as a family, a few women had some doubts about the wisdom of this. Some younger women also expressed the opinion that they would stop cruising and move ashore when they wanted to start a family.

June Macauley summed up the feelings of the most common age group, those cruising in their mid-thirties by saying, 'After being in the work force for many years, I really appreciate this life, whereas if I was older I might start running into problems of health or strength.' June should not have worried too much, as none of the ladies in their sixties found cruising life at all strenuous, stressing that age had not affected them at all.

The change of life style and environment had certainly affected these women more than their male partners and this was probably the reason why throughout the interviews they tended to make general comments, not relating just to themselves but to other seawives as well. Some of these comments, concerning marriage or the sharing of work, have been quoted earlier.

Suggestions for Others

At the end of each interview I asked the seawives if they wished to make some practical suggestions for the benefit of other women who intend to follow their example and set off on a long voyage. Dottie Fletcher, who both in port and at sea always has her hands full looking after her large family on board *Duen*, or helping with the maintenance work of this demanding boat, struck a realistic note when she advised potential seawives, 'Try and do some sailing even before you decide on buying a boat, it's a life you either love or you don't. There is nothing in between.' This is the reason why several women suggested that it was a good idea to go as crew or cruise on another boat to see what sailing offshore was all about. 'Charter for at least two weeks and make a passage of several days,' suggested Elizabeth Veuve of *Penelope*, who meant this advice for both men and women.

Although most seawives appeared to accept quite happily the absence of most conveniences of a modern home, some insisted on having at least a few basic comforts. Nancy Payson of *Sea Foam* was among these, and advised 'Try and have some comforts on your boat that are not too complicated. One spends so much time in the galley that one should try and have as many conveniences there as possible, like an oven, two sinks and, most important, a narrow and secure galley.'

Alice Simpson of *Fawn of Chichester*, an English girl fond of her cup of tea, pointed out that 'when cruising one spends in fact more time at anchor than at sea, so one shouldn't worry too much about breakable things, as it is so much nicer to drink out of ceramic mugs or glasses than plastic beakers.'

Several seawives stressed the importance of having their own interests and hobbies. Helga Seebeck, who had sailed around Cape Horn in the company of two male friends on the catamaran *Shangri-La*, insisted on her full share of all responsibilities on board. Her suggestion was 'Have another hobby besides sailing, that is, if sailing was your hobby in the first place.'

Brita Zeldenrust of *Kemana* was even more precise when she said 'Wives should have a hobby of their own; macramé, painting, fishing, studying birds, music, collecting shells, ham radio or writing. If such an interest is served by sailing or cruising, the better for it.'

Many of those interviewed took their hobbies very seriously or in the case of Kathy Becker of *Jocelyn*, her passion for amateur radio helped her put up with severe seasickness on long passages. Other women had special interests which they pursued while cruising, although reading was the favourite pastime. Marika Hantel of *Pytheas* took this seriously, making a point of reading about the history, political aspects, flora and fauna of the countries she sailed to. As a way of getting enjoyment out of the cruising life, several women mentioned meeting people or sightseeing, while three listed learning languages as one of their special interests, Margaret Pickering of *Keegenoo* being in the process of learning Tongan.

A lot of women had done work in the fitting out of their boats, from upholstery to sailmaking, while Madeleine Fily had done all the excellent woodwork in the interior of *Stereden Vor*. Many of these cruising wives also enjoyed snorkelling, diving and collecting shells. Several played a musical instrument, while others just enjoyed listening to music. A few took photographs seriously, painted or wrote, while Madeleine Gagnant of *Apoutziak* was especially interested in astronomy, the starry skies of the South Pacific providing much of interest. Not surprisingly, *Apoutziak* was one of the few boats on which star sights were taken regularly as part of the navigation routine.

Some suggestions were of a more practical nature, such as the one made by Barbara Dewey of *Hawk*: 'Acquire cookery books from the various countries. Try and cook dishes from strange places, otherwise you get tired of the same menu.' 'Stock up with good reference books on the places you intend to visit,' advised Alice Simpson of *Fawn of Chichester*, 'as these are not always available in the places themselves.' Two women wished they had learnt to can and preserve foods properly before they set off. Another one advised others to take along practical books on such matters as preserving food, while Pierrette Benoidt thought it essential to be able to bake one's own bread. Sylvia Beaurivage of *Drummer* had this advice: 'Read a lot of cruising books before you leave, to get an idea of what to expect.'

Rather than give suggestions, some women preferred to make a general comment on their present way of life, which, they hoped, could be of use to other women. 'A seawife is not a housewife afloat,' commented Stefani Stukenberg of *Orplid*, 'because on a boat the two partners depend so much more on each other. This is something a woman should consider carefully beforehand, as she is going to lead a life totally different from that ashore. On board she will never be just a wife.'

Even some of those wives who said that cruising had lived up to or even exceeded their expectations, were quick to point out the often unpleasant side of cruising and the danger of setting off with preconceived ideas. 'Don't think it is suburban life, because it isn't. You may have to get up at 3 am when the anchor drags,' was the sobering comment made by Beryl Allmark of *Telemark*.

Stefani and Rolf Stukenberg in happier days in Fiji before losing their *Orplid* on the Great Barrier Reef.

'Be ready to make your sacrifices, never to have your hair and nails done, and generally to be forced to work harder than at home,' said Kay Malseed of *Macushlah*, who nevertheless always managed to look smart and attractive.

But in spite of many disadvantages, as those mentioned by Kay or Beryl, several seawives emphasised that in the long run all these sacrifices were worthwhile.

In the end, what counted more than anything else appeared to be the wife's mental attitude, which was summed up by Marg Miller of *Galatea IV*, 'Prepare yourself mentally, as it is very important to have a positive attitude to this kind of life.' It is a view shared by Cristina Plantier of *Madame Bertrand*, 'Don't accept a passive role and think things are too difficult, but take an active interest in everything. There should be no difference between men and women on board a cruising boat.'

Ilse Gieseking of *Lou IV* was one of those who never had any doubts about the beauty of cruising life and when I asked for her suggestions she replied, 'If I gave some really good suggestions, the world's oceans would get overcrowded. If people only knew how beautiful this life can be, they would all set off, but they are too afraid.'

The overall conclusion I reached from my lengthy discussions with these seawives, several of whom have an outstanding record of ocean cruising behind them, is that the cruising life has innumerable rewards that far outweigh the inherent discomforts of life afloat. This observation is born out by the fact that most of the crews included in this survey planned to carry on cruising as long as possible, while many of those who were returning for various reasons to a land based existence, were already planning their next voyage. Most of these regarded settling back ashore with some trepidation. In many respects the sea had shown them what was truly essential in life, and this they often proposed to apply to their shorebound lives.

For a woman who takes up cruising as a way of life, the changes from a landbound existence are often greater than for a man, as are the mental and physical adaptations demanded of her. I certainly feel that if the man on board is aware of these demands and shows more understanding of the woman's different physical and mental makeup, the voyage stands a much better chance of success. Many men would do well to heed the sound advice of circumnavigator Herb Stewart of *Kyeri*, whose catchphrase for a successful cruise is 'Keep your wife happy.'

A Voyaging Woman

Many women participate fully in cruising and none more so than Ilse-Marie Gieseking, known as Illa to her many friends. I would even be so bold as to say that she was the driving force behind *Lou IV*'s successful circumnavigation. Illa always plays her full part in decision taking, route planning and does a considerable amount of the navigation. Like many couples who have sailed together for many years, the boatwork on *Lou IV* is evenly divided and runs smoothly, usually Illa being on the helm and Herbert on deck.

Many of the sailing wives I encountered were novices, but not Illa, for she has been sailing for over thirty years. The Giesekings have owned several boats previously, and sailing out of Elmshorn in Northern Germany over the years, they have cruised in the Baltic and the North Sea, visiting Scandinavia, the Orkneys and Shetland Islands, Scotland and England. But these trips satisfied them less and less and the temptation of a circumnavigation, something they had always dreamed of, became unbearable.

Illa was well used to making decisions, as for years she had run the business side of a small family firm, started by her grandfather, that made doors and window frames. She came to an agreement with her brother to look after things while she took off a few years for her dream cruise. Everything was so well organised on board *Lou IV*, that the voyage was bound to be a success. The 31 ft fibreglass ketch designed in Denmark by Jensen, was surprisingly roomy and well organised for its length, even having an aft cabin, although that was rather too hot and airless for the tropics. No job was ever postponed on *Lou IV* and the boat was impeccably maintained, returning home after four

Illa and Herbert Gieseking with their much loved friend Joshua Slocum.

and a half years and 46,000 miles with all original sails and hardly a scratch on the topsides.

Sailing a boat in tip-top condition and with their long experience, it is not surprising that the voyage exceeded Illa's expectations. Although following the normal trade wind route, or as Illa calls it 'the route of least resistance', they did however make some notable detours. The longest was to sail the entire eastern seaboard of the United States to Canada, up the St Lawrence river into the Great Lakes and back down the Eyrie barge canal and Hudson river to New York. They were also one of the few cruising boats to venture south and cruise off New Zealand's South Island. In Illa's opinion that was the toughest cruising they had ever experienced, worse than the North Sea with wild weather, strong currents, and deep anchorages where the wind screamed down the mountains. The lonely grandeur of the scenery was the only compensation. Apart from a soft spot for Moorea, Illa's favourite cruising ground was the Solomon Islands, which she found to be unspoilt and little visited by tourists or yachts.

Illa's constant companion on the cruise was a small black poodle called Joshua Slocum. Although she loves him dearly and finds him a great pleasure at sea, she admits it was a mistake taking him with them, for it restricted their visits ashore in many places. Illa's warm expansive character extended to children too, as mine were quick to discover and exploit, as Illa never failed to produce a piece of chocolate when they paid her a visit.

Reluctantly the Giesekings turned *Lou IV*'s bow back from the Pacific towards Europe, for Illa could not leave her brother holding the fort for too long. Then tragedy struck them, their only son being killed in a road accident in Germany, unbeknown to them while they were on the long passage from Capetown to the Azores. Illa now had lost any interest she had in keeping the business going. Life ashore suddenly seemed hollow, with nothing to work for and no one to pass on to. She also found that the years at sea had changed her and she now had a different attitude to life than the people around her. What had seemed important before no longer mattered.

There were pleasures on their return home, seeing old friends and a splendid welcome by their yacht club. They also received the Kronenkompass, the highest cruising award of the German Cruising Club. In her typical efficient way, Illa wrote, published and sold her own book of their cruise. The pleasures however soon began to pall and there was only one solution as far as Illa was concerned, to leave again and this time for as long as she and Herbert were physically able. *Lou IV* was sold soon afterwards and replaced with *Lou V*, a 40 ft steel ketch built to the Giesekings' exact specifications by a small Danish firm of boatbuilders. Once the decision to set sail again was taken, Illa folded up her share of the family business, leaving it all to her brother. In the summer of 1984 the Giesekings were on the move again, only this time they have decided to take their time. Having completed one circumnavigation, the urge to rush around the world is gone and they plan to spend several years exploring the Mediterranean before venturing farther afield.

When I asked Illa about the right age for cruising, her answer was very clear.

'Starting younger would have been better, then I would have gone around the world three times. Now I only have time left for twice. In my next life, if I have a choice, I shall do the sailing first and work later.' Yet in her usual, efficient way, Illa seems to have organised plenty of sailing in her present life.

CHAPTER SEVEN
Cruising with Children

Children on cruising boats are no longer the exception, as more and more families, who undertake long voyages, take their children with them. Cruising with children does present certain problems however, and in my second survey of long distance cruising boats one section dealt exclusively with questions concerning children. Out of fifty boats, eight had children on board, and I also questioned a ninth boat, on which the 17-year old was already playing a full part as an adult member of the crew. On five boats the children were single, the remaining four having two children each. The ages varied from three to seventeen, the majority being in the eight to thirteen year old group.

Small boat harbour on Raiatea, in the Society Islands.

In the Pacific survey the increase in families cruising was remarkable, nearly one third of the boats having children in the crew. In total there were twenty children on fourteen boats, ranging in age from 6 months to 16 years. Again, I questioned these parents on various aspects of cruising with children.

Growing Up Afloat

Most parents considered that their children's general attitude to life at sea was good, some describing it as perfect or pointing out that, as the children had virtually grown up at sea, they took boat life for granted, regarding it as the normal thing. Children seem to adapt much more easily than adults to living in a watery environment and this perhaps was the reason why heavy weather did not bother most of the children, many carrying on with their activities as in normal weather. Several parents mentioned that during bad weather children went to sleep and slept soundly through anything, although sometimes taking to the main cabin floor, especially when their normal bunks were in the fo'c'sle.

The few parents who had reservations were all those with younger children. Vicki Holmes of *Korong II* admitted that it was a strain cruising with two small children, but she hoped that it would improve when the children were old enough to give the parents some time to call their own and it was not necessary to permanently watch what the children were up to. After a two year cruise, Vicki and John Holmes did return home. Another couple with a child in this pre-school age group was Sylvia and Ian French of *Pomona* among the dozen circumnavigators I interviewed later. Keeping young John occupied and amused took up most of the parents' time, both in port and on passage.

In the Pacific survey Nina and Juan Ribas of *Abuelo III* thought sailing was a hard life for small children, as they could not understand why they were not allowed to play with the controls of certain attractive things like the autopilot or amateur radio, nor could they understand why parents were more nervous and had less time for them when the weather was bad. Several parents mentioned a minimum age of five and considered older children appreciated the voyage more, the under-fives needing too much attention and lacking interest in the places visited.

Occupying older children while on long passages was easier, with reading being the favourite pastime. Most cruising children read a lot, one of them devouring a book almost every day. Obtaining an adequate supply of reading material, especially in smaller places was often a major problem, although the children themselves often overcame this by swapping books with those on other boats. Games and puzzles were also popular, children close in age played a great deal together, while others drew, painted or listened to special cassettes with stories and music, especially in bad weather. Some of the parents made special preparations for a passage, such as buying new toys, games, books or story and music cassettes. On longer passages, these were often kept hidden and produced at intervals. Other parents recommended that it was important a child had plenty of playing space, where constructions and games could be left and not dismantled. One mother suggested a completely separate cabin was essential, which could be left in a mess at sea, so that the children felt at home and could play without interfering with the routine of the boat.

All the children helped out with jobs to a lesser or greater extent, even five year olds doing simple things like tidying up and coiling ropes. Eight year olds would progress to washing up or handling the jib sheets in normal weather. Most children over eleven participated fully in life aboard, some of them being given precise jobs, while others helped out generally. All the older children also stood watches when at sea. Two children, aged eight and ten, on different boats, had to do an hour watch in the daytime. On *Fortuna*, Paul and Tina Morrish, thirteen and eleven at the time of the survey, had been keeping

On *Pytheas* dad's work bench is easily converted to a Lego construction table.

full watches for some time and as the boat had no selfsteering, they had to steer by hand day and night, whatever the weather. On *Sea Foam*, seventeen year old Craig had been taking a full day watch from the age of ten and also a night watch from the age of fourteen.

In every case the children living afloat did appear to be mature and responsible for their age. Linda Balcombe of *Starshine* pointed out that her eleven year old daughter Heather had matured considerably compared with her peer group as a result of living in an adult world. 'I think it is a good life for these children, they see a lot of the world and it can't help but be an improvement.'

Although the majority of parents considered that the voyage had benefited the child in many ways, from learning other languages to opening their eyes on the world, several parents had doubts about forcing a child into an adult environment.

'It's very easy for a child to become an adult without ever being a child,' said Bernard Tournier of *Volte*, counselling parents to take two children cruising for this reason, never one alone. This same advice was given by the Brysons cruising on *Ave del Mar* with their twelve-year-old son Stuart. Marge Bryson balanced the benefits of the voyage for Stuart – an increased independence, self sufficiency and a respect for the forces of nature – against the disadvantages, namely living in an adult world, which resulted in social problems when Stuart had to adjust to being with other children again. Stuart himself considered the lack of other children his age the biggest drawback to life afloat, but one he readily accepted for the other pleasures of the cruising life. All the family agreed that a few years younger would have been a preferable age.

Education

Education is one of the major concerns of all parents taking their children out of the school system for any length of time and none of those surveyed had neglected this aspect. Many of the children were using a correspondence course from their country of origin, which meant that it would be easier for them to rejoin their particular system if and when they returned ashore later on.

The Calvert School correspondence course was used on five American boats, which they all found to be satisfactory. Only one parent qualified this praise by saying that although the system was good for the basic skills at a lower age, she had some reservations about the later grades and particularly the science subjects needed supplementing. Another parent, who considered the Calvert excellent value for money, chose, however, not to send the work back for correction.

The return of completed work for correction was one of the major problems encountered by all those using correspondence courses, as reliable mailing addresses were rare and the mailing of material to and from remote places was erratic and unpredictable. The children had often forgotten about the work by the time it arrived back with marks and comments, which was especially true in the case of younger children. This was a particular bugbear for the yacht *Calao*, who used the state system provided free by the French government. As schooling of French children is compulsory, regardless of where they are, it meant that a large amount of work had to be sent back regularly, the rigid requirements of the scheme being a great strain on both the children and their parents. Several times they had to delay their departure from a port, waiting for new course work to arrive. As well as being rigid, they found the system difficult to adapt to the cruising way of life.

More flexible state systems were highly praised by their users including those provided by Alaska, New Zealand and Australia. The Australian state of Queensland course is one of the most comprehensive, being sent out with cassettes and slides. A science kit for experiments is also available, but has to be picked up as the chemicals cannot be posted overseas. Ronald and Edith van Zelderen on *White Pointer* have been using this course for eight years on their circumnavigation and now on their second voyage. Sixteen-year-old Ronald, who, apart from a year at school in Holland, has completed all his education afloat, was preparing to take his School Certificate exams at the Australian consulate in Tahiti. As their mother Maria remarked, 'The system is good, but everything depends on the effort the student is prepared to put into it.' On *White Pointer*, Ronald and Edith did their school work in different cabins, so as not to distract each other. Their mother thought that the effort needed to keep the schoolwork going was considerable, but had to be faced or real problems could arise.

Some parents had solved the problem of both the relevance of the material and the marking of it, by devising their own system of education. Liz MacDonald of *Horizon*, who is a qualified teacher, educated her son Jeff entirely by herself during their three year long circumnavigation. Liz tried hard to keep the material relevant, for example in Fiji, where I spoke to her, she was teaching from a book of Pacific history used in the local schools. Throughout the voyage, Liz conscientiously kept an exact record of all the work, Jeff's behaviour and attitude, as well as his marks. She found it essential to stick to a daily routine and definite timetable, an absolute requirement also pointed out by other teaching parents. The discipline involved in educating children at sea was considered by many parents as one of the most trying and difficult aspects of cruising.

It is no wonder then that many parents happily sent their children off to local schools whenever a stay in port was long enough to warrant this. On the other hand, two boats using the Calvert system never sent the children to school ashore, so as not to interrupt the course unnecessarily, while the children on another boat only went to school in English speaking countries. Some of the parents however used the chance offered by travelling in foreign lands for their children to learn another language. This is why Sidonie and Fabien of *Calao* speak English with a broad Australian accent and my own children used to speak French with a Polynesian twang picked up after one month of school on Mangareva in French Polynesia.

Another reason some parents gave for sending their children to local schools was the chance to make contact and mix with children of their own age. Some of the sailing children made friends only slowly with children ashore, although more easily with children on other boats. About half of the children however, who had got used to their peripatetic life, had learned to make friends at lightning speed, knowing that time was short and soon they would be on the move again.

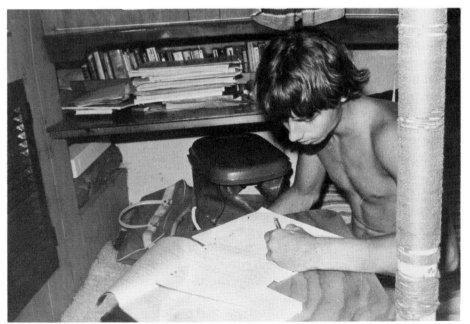

After completing most of his education afloat, sixteen-year-old Ronald van Zelderen works towards his final examinations.

As the children progress into teenage, this need for friends of similar age becomes more acute and their schooling also gets increasingly difficult. Several of these families planned to end their cruise before their children got too old and were thinking of staying ashore for a few years while the children completed their education. The thirteen year old on one of the boats surveyed was eventually dispatched home to attend school. Other boats with children on board which I have met over the years, but were not included in this survey, had run into similar problems. After using correspondence courses for a while, one French couple decided to send their two teenage children home to boarding school, aiming to cruise in convenient places where the children could join them during their holidays. Neither parents nor children were too happy with this arrangement, so after a year the boat was sold in Singapore, the cruise abandoned and the entire family returned to France. A New Zealand couple also found it very difficult to get their teenager to apply himself to school work and eventually sent him home ahead of them. Unfortunately the parents found that he never caught up with his age group and left school discontented and with a feeling of inferiority.

Most of the points raised here I know only too well from personal experience, my children Doina and Ivan being seven and five when we left England and thirteen and eleven when we returned six years later. Like Liz MacDonald, my wife Gwenda qualified as a teacher as part of the long term preparations for our cruise, and devised a personal education for our children. They studied Greek history and legends in the Aegean, the Bible stories in Israel, the history of the slave trade in the West Indies and discussed Thor Heyerdahl's theories on the way to Easter Island. Whenever possible we sent the children to school ashore, even for as little as two days on Pitcairn Island. We found schools everywhere to be very welcoming and friendly and their teachers seemed to value the window on the outside world that Doina and Ivan were able to open to the children in such remote communities.

We had originally planned to be back on land for their secondary education, but we all enjoyed life afloat so much that our cruise was extended. As Doina reached thirteen, Gwenda found it more and more difficult to cope with teaching all subjects and she subscribed to correspondence courses from the National Extension College in Cambridge. Although designed primarily for adults, the courses seemed perfectly suited for an older child, as much of the work was self-marked and the assignments did not have to be sent back to the tutor too frequently, a great advantage for the student continually on the move. On returning to England after more than six years afloat we were pleased to find that the children were at no disadvantage academically, but in fact had a great richness of experience to draw on. Not jaded by years in a classroom, they had a more positive attitude towards learning than many of their peers, especially in the subjects that interested them. At the beginning they experienced some difficulty fitting in socially, as they stood out as being different, but this problem resolved itself as time passed and they made new friends.

Taking children out of the system and educating them afloat is perfectly possible, but does require a great amount of effort, patience and above all discipline, both from parents and children. Gwenda regards schooling as being by far the most demanding and time consuming aspect of our voyage, a point of view shared by most parents. It is the price one has to pay.

Sylvia and Ian French, who left with son John aged twenty months on a three year long circumnavigation on *Pomona*, planned to be back home by the time John was due to start school. On their return however they did not regard this aspect to be as crucial as they had originally thought, and would consider taking him out of school if they made another voyage.

Infants Aboard

Schooling may be a headache to many parents, but having toddlers on board is not easy either, as they require constant supervision and the parents cannot properly relax until the child can swim. At the bottom end of the scale, small babies thrive quite happily in the salty atmosphere of a rocking boat. Derry Hancock of *Runestaff* gave birth to Tristan in Suva at the time of my first survey and at the age of only six weeks Tristan made the 1000 mile passage to New Zealand quite happily, although the Hancocks did take an extra crew to give them a hand. Water babies suddenly seemed the fashion, as several cruising boats increased their crews the following year. This often raised the question of the new arrival's nationality and passport, and the new parents had variable amounts of difficulty trying to sort out this problem with their respective embassies.

In the Pacific survey I was surprised to find that eleven of the children could not swim properly, although this included mainly the younger children, some of whom were in the process of learning. That age need not be a bar was shown by 6-year old Nicky Samuelson of *Swan II*, who has been swimming since she was 7 months old. On only one of the boats did the children wear a harness or lifejacket all the time, while another couple of non-swimmers wore harnesses at sea, but not in port, their parents saying they were always vigilant. One young non-swimmer wore a life jacket some of the time, for example when alone in the dinghy with his elder brother. Yet I was amazed to hear that one of the non-swimmers had already had been fished out of the harbour twice in Papeete and still his parents did not insist on a lifejacket or harness, nor did they appear to be making any effort to teach him to swim. In

Luisa Ribas is never without a buoyancy aid while on deck on *Abuelo III*.

my opinion, teaching a child to swim is one of the priorities for parents living afloat.

Max Fletcher had higher than average stanchions on his Westsail 32 and high netting all the way around the boat, still always keeping a careful eye on his young son. Many parents stressed that their children usually stayed below at sea, especially if the weather was bad, and were always under supervision in the cockpit. On *Pytheas* the side of the wheelhouse could be closed off, so that the children could not get out of the cockpit. Even older children were not usually allowed on deck at sea.

Few of the parents sailing with children regretted their decision to take the family with them to sea. Many mentioned that it brought about a closeness in their family life, which they had rarely experienced before. It was also pointed out that the fathers were far more involved with bringing up their children than when the family had been living ashore, with the father only seeing the children for a few hours a day, whereas on a boat the family was together all the time. The presence of children also guaranteed a warmer reception in most communities and even officials visiting a boat tended to be more friendly when children were about.

A few parents had some misgivings about taking their children cruising, mainly for the lack of social contact with other children. It was clear that many parents had thought deeply about this whole question. Monique and Bernard Tournier of *Volte* had taken some time after launching their boat in preparing their children for the voyage, spending the summers sailing and the winters ashore, waiting for the childen to grow up. In the earlier survey, some of the older children were not too happy about living such a close family life and had more reservations than their parents, yet in the Pacific survey the older children were more positive, often adding that they would willingly go cruising again. Among those with small children, many parents had no complaints.

'It has been much easier cruising with a small child than I thought it would be,' said Max Fletcher of *Christopher Robin*. Yet from the consensus of views expressed by both children and parents, it would appear that family cruising is at its most successful after the children have grown out of infancy and before adolescence.

Much depends on the parents' attitude, as Dorine Samuelson of *Swan II* remarked, 'If the parents are happy and enjoying the sailing life, the children will be happy and like it too.' Or as Jean-Pierre Martin of *El Djezair* put it, 'It's very simple to leave, so one should not look for complications.' From the increasing number of families successfully cruising the oceans, it is plain that this is a sentiment felt by many.

Derry Hancock took motherhood in her stride and before baby Tristan was six weeks old, he had successfully completed a 1000 mile passage from Fiji to New Zealand.

CHAPTER EIGHT

Long Term Planning

A long and successful ocean cruise is invariably the result of careful planning. Sometimes it takes years to arrange all aspects of shore life so that it is finally possibly to cast off. However, it is by no means always true that exact routes and schedules must be adhered to slavishly: one of the virtues of good cruise planning is to allow for flexibility and improvisation if necessary. Unexpected delays and diversions can occur, and the true meaning of good planning is therefore preparation for a variety of options. The truth of this is well underlined by the experiences of two boats I encountered during my own circumnavigation – the MacDonalds on *Horizon* and the Bouteleux on *Calao*. Their stories are both object lessons in different ways, and on the following pages a brief outline follows:

The MacDonalds' Five-year Plan

Life in rural New England for Bruce MacDonald was dull, as he struggled to support his wife Liz and baby son Jeff on a ski-instructor's income. He avidly read true adventure stories, whether mountain climbing or deep sea diving, polar expeditions or safaris across Africa. The books only made it worse for the young couple and the future seemed as bleak and dull as the present. Climbing Mount Everest or trekking to the North Pole looked impossible, but to sail away across the oceans was one dream they felt might be possible to fulfil one day. They drew up a five year plan and that alone injected a new purpose and challenge into their daily routine.

Reading every book they could find about sailing and ocean cruising, the MacDonalds started planning. They soon realised that the first requirement was a good reliable boat and raising the capital for that was their biggest hurdle. So the young couple put their five year plan into action. They both took better paid teaching jobs and started saving. To raise the capital they set about building a house in their spare time, doing all the building, carpentry, plumbing and heating themselves, hoping that the eventual sale of the house would provide the funds for their boat.

MAP E Most popular routes for circumnavigators taking advantage of prevailing winds

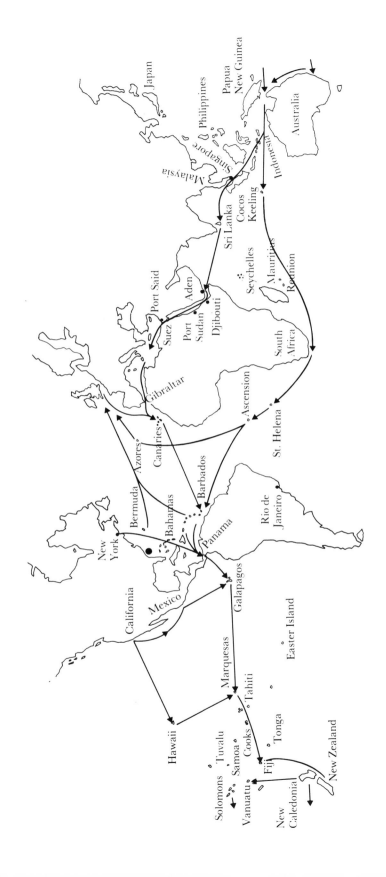

To learn about sailing they acquired a 14 ft sailing dinghy, which they took on long trips to Lake Champlain. Bruce had learned navigation and much about the sea as watch officer on a destroyer in the US navy during his military service, so at least in one province they did not have to start from scratch.

Meanwhile they worked and saved every cent, although often they had serious doubts that their dream would ever become reality. Then in 1977, they sold everything they possessed and were able to buy *Horizon*, a secondhand Golden Hind sloop. That still left them enough savings over to live modestly for a few years afloat. The 31 ft Golden Hind was the best boat they could afford and they regarded the fibreglass sheathed plywood hull as sturdy enough to take them across the oceans.

I first met the MacDonalds in Beaufort, North Carolina, while they were waiting for a break in the weather to embark on their first long ocean passage. It is difficult for experienced skippers, let alone for novices, to judge the right moment to leave from the United States for the Caribbean. An early departure means running the risk of a late hurricane or tropical depression, while the later it gets into winter, the greater the chance of strong northerly gales which, blowing against the three knot current of the Gulf Stream, chop up treacherous swell conditions. I left in early November and had to skirt a tropical depression, fortunately tracked accurately by the US weather bureau, whereas the MacDonalds' later passage to Puerto Rico tested their endurance to the utmost. With constant northerlies of 40 knots and over, they broke gear, blew out the mainsail and nearly lost their mast. In Puerto Rico they discovered that the mast had compressed and buckled nearly four inches at the base and had to be unstepped, cut and re-fitted. However, they were not daunted by their rough baptism and carried on with their plan of cruising the Caribbean, telling themselves that these were all unavoidable teething problems caused by their lack of experience and hasty preparations. Bruce and Liz soon discovered that the cruising life exceeded their expectations and that in spite of all difficulties it was worth carrying on. The possibility of a world voyage had always been in the back of their minds, so they took the plunge. They went through the Panama Canal and headed west.

Bearded Bruce is as tall as petite Liz is tiny, but both agree that cruising has brought a closeness to their family life. Bruce feels that for son Jeff to see his parents coping with real stress situations only benefits a child and they have had their share of those, such as when Liz had to be hoisted up the mast at sea to replace a broken halyard.

As both parents are qualified teachers, they opted to teach Jeff themselves, although this became mainly Liz's duty. In her thorough way she applied herself to this mammoth task with great discipline, teaching Jeff the history

The MacDonalds on
Horizon proved that
determination can make
anything possible.

and geography of all the places visited. Using the environment of tropical vegetation and coral reefs provided nature study, whilst they kept his mathematics up to scratch. She kept a meticulous record of everything she did and made sure that no aspect of Jeff's education was overlooked.

Their budget had to be equally meticulous, as their limited savings meant they had to plan and watch every cent. With inflation and rising prices the budget got tighter and tighter as the voyage progressed. At least a chance of work in New Zealand allowed them to replace *Horizon*'s doubtful mast before crossing the Indian and Atlantic oceans. Their tight budget did not stop them enjoying life and following their particular hobby of walking and mountaineering. They trekked across many of the islands on foot, the high impenetrable Marquesas being one of their favourite places.

In 1980 after sailing 34,000 miles, they had the great satisfaction of accomplishing what they had set out to do, to circumnavigate the globe. The MacDonalds are for me the best example to be given to all those who say

'Aren't you lucky', for they have shown how much hard work, determination and planning are needed. And how little depends on being lucky.

Like many parents who would prefer to remain afloat but cannot do it, Bruce and Liz have settled ashore until teenage Jeff has finished his education, but a new plan was already taking shape before they even settled down ashore. Cruising life has cast a permanent spell on the MacDonalds, for immediately they started planning another world voyage. Like other circumnavigators, Bruce chose a steel cutter, the Departure 35, designed by Charles Wittholz as his ideal boat, not only because it fulfilled most parameters he had set himself, but also because it could be bought as a bare hull from a builder in the Chesapeake. After two years of hard work fitting out the hull in their backyard, the MacDonalds are once again ready to set sail for new horizons.

Rendezvous with Calao

It began quite early in our circumnavigation of the world. A blond fellow of my own age was watching us from the cockpit of his boat, as we edged *Aventura*'s stern towards the Yacht Club wall after having dropped anchor in Santa Cruz de la Palma. Seeing all the other boats had a stern line to the wall, I started preparing a long line to take ashore.

'If you desire my dinghy, you can have her!' I heard the chap shout across from his boat.

'No thanks, I have to launch mine anyway,' I replied, trying to suppress my amusement at his unintentional *double entendre*.

'I'll come and aid you,' he said with a brilliant smile, and without waiting for a reply, jumped into the object of my rejected desire and with a hefty shove brought himself alongside *Aventura*.

'I am Erick Bouteleux . . . from France,' he added, unnecessarily, as from his unmistakeable accent I had already guessed that he could not possibly hail from anywhere else.

So started a long friendship between our two crews, nurtured by countless hours of cockpit chatter under balmy tropical skies, joint spearfishing or fruit gathering expeditions for Erick and I, exchange of schooling and cooking tips between Muriel and Gwenda, and ear-splitting discussions in atrocious Franglais between Sidonie, Fabien, Doina and Ivan, while *Calao* and *Aventura* reeled off thousands of miles cruising in company.

We met again in Barbados, where *Calao* arrived after an excellent crossing of only eighteen days from the Canaries, which however had been beset by a series of serious failures, not totally unexpected on a wooden boat nearly a quarter of a century old. The swift 40 ft Finisterre class yawl had been built to the high specifications of her original American owner by a Portuguese yard in 1953. By the time Erick bought her in La Havre, *Calao* had been badly neglected, but her elegant lines appealed to him so much, that he fell in love with her and within two years declared her ready to take on the oceans of the world. He folded up his successful insurance agency and with wife Muriel, daughter Sidonie, who was five at the time and son Fabien, only two, they set off on a long voyage which both Erick and Muriel wanted to do and enjoy while they were still young.

During the first winter of cruising in the Caribbean we often met by chance, until one evening when I described my plans of visiting the United States during the hurricane season in the Caribbean.

'That sounds very tempting,' replied Erick, who until then had been thinking of spending the season somewhere completely different. Obviously a detour of several thousand miles meant nothing to him, something that he later demonstrated on several occasions. He could change long established

The crew of *Calao* having fun in Vava'u, Tonga. Muriel is swiftly lifted out of the water by *Calao*'s 1000 sq ft spinnaker.

plans at the drop of a hat and, with his infectious enthusiasm, never had any trouble in getting Muriel to go along with the change. I soon found that Erick was game for any hairbrained idea, as long as it was crazy enough, such as night diving for lobster, salvaging useless stuff from sunken wrecks, crossing New York on folding bicycles, or spinnaker flying over an anchorage constantly visited by sharks. Anchoring *Calao* by the stern the spi-rider sat in the bosun's chair attached to the spinnaker, which let out on the halyard billows out like a parachute over the water.

'Having a fixed itinerary and then sticking to it, is about the most stupid thing one can do in this free life of ours,' he once said, while we were discussing which route to take after the United States and the Caribbean. I had already told him of my intention to sail down the coast of South America to Peru and thence to Easter Island. 'Oh, no, that's one place you won't find me,' he replied firmly. 'I have absolutely no desire to battle with the strength of the Humboldt current, when I can have an easy sail to the Marquesas.' We parted wakes in North Carolina, not sure when we would meet again, as we were planning to move at a faster rate than *Calao*. I was not too surprised however to discover that *Calao* had followed us to Peru, the temptation of seeing that part of the world being irresistible to such globe trotters as Erick and Muriel.

After spending the cyclone season in New Zealand, we decided to stay another year in the South Pacific and make a long detour to be in Tarawa for the Gilbert Islands' Independence Celebrations. By letter Erick and I decided *Aventura*'s track from New Zealand to the Gilberts could well intercept *Calao*'s track from Tahiti to Australia and we chose a suitable rendezvous in Vava'u, Tonga. We surpassed even our own expectations by arriving at the rendezvous only two hours apart.

Not having seen each other for over a year we easily filled the days swapping tales and gently cruising among the many islands of the Tongan archipelago. Work and mail however was waiting for me in Western Samoa, so I tried to persuade the Bouteleux to sail there as well, promising to take them out to dinner at Aggie Grey's famous hotel to celebrate Gwenda's birthday.

The weather was bad as we sailed out of Vava'u with headwinds and the promise of worse to come. On one of the tacks we got close enough together for me to shout across to Erick, that as they had recently sailed down from Samoa, they should carry on west and wait for us in Wallis, as they had originally planned. As darkness fell we lost sight of *Calao*. It took us five days of hard unpleasant sailing to cover the 300 odd miles to reach Samoa, so later the same day I couldn't believe it when *Calao* swept into Apia under full sail.

'Why on earth did you fight your way here, when you could have had a pleasant sail to Wallis?' I shouted across to Erick, incapable of hiding my surprise. It was his turn to look surprised.

'But, Jimmy, didn't you invite me to dinner? Surely you don't think we would miss an invitation to Aggie Grey's, do you?' At least it was worth the passage, as the same evening we sat down to an excellent dinner in the unique atmosphere of Aggie Grey's, the best known hotel in the South Pacific, run with unparalleled panache by this spritely lady eighty years young.

In Wallis, we separated again, this time agreeing to meet the following year in Australia. It was a meeting *Calao* almost never made. While sailing from Wallis to Futuna, two French territories in the Central Pacific, *Calao* encountered bad weather with mountainous seas. She fell into a deep trough and split a seam, the boat barely making the lee of Futuna with water gushing in through the open seam.

While *Aventura* spent the following cyclone season in Papua New Guinea, *Calao* chose the dry climate of Queensland so that Erick could restore his wooden decks. We arranged to meet in Cairns and sail to join an armada of traditional canoes sailing along the coast of Papua to Port Moresby as part of the Pacific Festival of Arts.

It was late on the day of our rendezvous when I saw the familiar shape of *Calao* down the river at Cairns. The boat seemed to be making very slow progress and then I saw that Erick was sitting in his Optimist dinghy and with his small outboard motor towing *Calao* behind him. I jumped in my dinghy to help.

'What has happened?' I asked.

'Oh, nothing much, we had to buck the current as the tide was running out. The oil pressure warning lamp came on, but as we were in the middle of the narrow channel with so much shipping, I didn't stop the engine. So it seized up.' Erick shrugged his shoulders. 'Still I kept the rendezvous, didn't I?'

Closer inspection at anchor revealed that without oil, the engine had well and truly seized up. He also discovered that he could not get the spare parts for his Peugeot engine in Australia and that they would have to be ordered from France. Erick is not easily daunted.

'We'll opt out of following the Armada in and out of the reef along the Papuan coast, but I don't want to miss the Festival, so we will sail straight to Port Moresby. If Captain Cook could sail up the Barrier reef without an engine, so can I.' I refrained from pointing out that we were not all that far from where Cook's *Endeavour* ran aground, and *Calao* sailed uneventfully the 500 miles to Port Moresby, where the spare parts eventually arrived from Paris. At least Erick absolved himself for his grave error of disregarding the warning lamp, by repairing and reassembling the engine completely unaided. His unique talent of improvisation had always impressed me, hardly any job being too difficult for his well stocked workshop, set up in the oversized sail locker in

Calao's bows. In spite of the tremendous amount of maintenance work required by such an old wooden boat, *Calao* was always kept in spotless condition with gleaming topsides and brilliantly varnished spars.

Far from being a purist in the true sense of the word, Erick is a perfectionist when it comes to sailing his boat. Although equipped with selfsteering and an autopilot, on passage he rarely reads and likes to spend his time sitting in the cockpit physically enjoying the sailing and the water rushing past the hull. He sails the 40 ft *Calao* as though he was in a dinghy race. The sails are always perfectly trimmed for maximum efficiency and when the wind drops, up goes the 1000 sq ft spinnaker, *Calao* being one of the few cruising boats on which a spinnaker is constantly used. It is the one sail, for which the entire crew has to lend a hand, while young Sidonie and Fabien have sole responsibility for the mizzen staysail.

The childrens' education has taxed both parents to the limit, especially in the case of Fabien, who had no idea of school discipline and regarded the boat and the sea as his natural playground. While his son was younger, Erick had rigged a continuous wire around the wide side decks, along which Fabien, attached to the wire by his harness, would run incessantly like a dog on a lead, working off his excess energy. When he reached the age of five, morning play had to give way to school work, a daily task the purpose of which Fabien refused to comprehend. On many mornings I could hear Erick's exasperated voice booming across the anchorage. 'Two and three make five. Five, do you understand? Five, like the fingers on your hand, you twit!'

Two terms in an Australian school, while Erick and Muriel prepared *Calao* for the long return to Europe, did wonders for the childrens' education. It also brought about an odd change, for they ceased to speak French to each other and would argue incessantly with a genuine Aussie twang.

As the children grew and Sidonie started approaching secondary school age, a return to France became a prospect which could no longer be ignored. *Calao*'s westward track became less erratic and after leaving Torres Straits behind, *Calao* headed for Indonesia, and yet another rendezvous with *Aventura*. We had already been sailing for over one month among the Indonesian islands and had arrived one week before the agreed date in Bali. On the appointed day, not expecting Bouteleux to yet again show up on time, we had already locked up the boat and were preparing to go ashore when *Calao* sailed slowly into Benoa. They dropped anchor next to us and when Erick saw that we were all packed up ready to go, called across,

'Give us ten minutes and we'll come too.'

'No hurry,' I replied, 'take your time, we can go tomorrow.'

'Why tomorrow? What's wrong with today?'

Indeed within ten minutes they were all ashore ready to join us in a three day trip of the interior of the island, as if they had just sailed across the bay and not a distance of over 1000 miles. There are many outstanding people among the cruising fraternity and Erick Bouteleux is only one of them, but whatever other qualities he may have, he certainly knows how to keep an appointment.

Calao leaving Singapore at the beginning of a long cruise in the Indian Ocean.

A Final Word

The stories interspersed among the foregoing chapters describe only a handful of people, whose personal experiences were considered to illustrate a particular point. In fact, the number of outstanding people whom I have met during my travels was far greater and I am able to present only the quintessence of their knowledge in these pages. As Eric Hiscock told me himself, however much one knows about the sea and sailing, one can still learn a lot from others; so I have been the first person to benefit from the information and suggestions that came my way. While such tips and advice have been of great use to me in a practical way, the attitudes of certain sailors have greatly influenced my own way of thinking and looking at things. My first mentor was the Italian singlehander Mario Franchetti, whose boat *Coconasse* was a perfect example of effortless sailing combined with maximum comfort and security. Albert Steele and Mike Bailes have taught me the virtue of patience, while Susan and Eric Hiscock that of modesty. From Chester Lemon I learned that on a boat, nothing should be impossible and everything can be fixed, while Erick and Muriel Bouteleux have shown me more than once the true meaning of friendship.

In an increasingly impersonal world, it is reassuring to see the great generosity shown by many members of the cruising fraternity to each other. Ashore too there are still many people in various parts of the world, who shower their generosity upon the crews of visiting boats, usually without expecting anything in return. They are proud to be hosts to a fellow human being who has had the courage to set off across the oceans in a small boat to visit their distant shores. However, with more and more people taking to the sea, a long voyage by small boat is no longer regarded such an unusual feat as to merit special recognition and the reception given to the voyager is often becoming less enthusiastic.

This is an aspect which I have discussed at length with some of the older crews, who can still remember, with justified nostalgia, the days when they hardly ever had to share an anchorage with another boat and were received everywhere with the utmost warmth and friendliness. These sailors also pointed to a gradual change that has occurred over recent years in small boat voyagers, from seafarers to sightseers. More and more people take to the sea as a means of seeing the world and not just for the love of sailing. The one thing they have in common, sailors and tourists alike, is still the mode of transport and because of that, certain rules of the sea have to be obeyed by all. A desire to see the world is certainly a valid reason for putting to sea in a small boat, as long as the basic tenets of seamanship and navigation are not ignored.

What I feel is wrong is to bring to the sea some of the attitudes of modern mass tourism. Although the majority of voyagers behave in a responsible and considerate fashion, there are unfortunately a few whose attitudes towards both officials and locals in foreign countries spoil the scene for all those who follow behind. It is mostly these selfish attitudes which have brought about the change deplored by those who were fortunate enough to cruise the world two or three decades ago. The reception given by local people is often less friendly than in the past, while some yacht clubs will no longer extend the customary hospitality to visiting crews, usually because someone had left with unpaid bills or had abused club facilities.

An even more disturbing trait that is noticeable among a few sailing people, apart from a lack of honesty and consideration, is that of racial prejudice. I was stunned to hear a skipper call the immigration officer in Tahiti 'boy', or a young sailor refer to customs officers in Sri Lanka as 'stupid niggers'. During a traditional welcoming ceremony in Fiji, the crew of one yacht refused to shake hands with the island chief, because he was black, after which the attitude of the villagers towards all visitors became markedly cool. In a small port in Malaysia it took only one skipper to insult an immigration official and two years later visiting crews could still not get more than a two week extension to their visas, while elsewhere they could get up to three months. It does indeed take only a few such rotten apples to spoil the barrel for all of us who follow in their wake. Such examples have only been included to show that having a sound boat and being a good sailor does not preclude the need to also have a large amount of commonsense and consideration for others.

Commonsense is something that should dictate not only one's relationship with people on other boats and ashore, but also the kind of boat one chooses and the way everything is prepared for the intended voyage. The choice of boat is one area where a wrong decision can put the entire voyage in jeopardy later on. Unfortunately it is one decision which by necessity most people have to make before acquiring the cruising experience, which may well dictate new priorities. It is the reason why so many skippers stressed the overriding importance of trying to get one's priorities right from the begining. I should point out perhaps that most of the people I interviewed are the success stories, which were often matched by at least an equal number of failures and abandoned voyages. The wrong type of boat was often specified as the prime cause of such failures. It is a pitfall however that can be avoided by considering carefully from the beginning two important factors, the age and size of the crew and the area to be cruised.

Too small a boat with a crew that includes small children, can become unacceptably crammed as the voyage progresses and the children are growing. Similarly too large a boat for those who may lose part of the crew en route, or may become physically less able to handle it as they get older, can be equally frustrating.

The area where one is likely to spend most of the time should also have a bearing on the choice of boat. If one plans to follow the trade wind route around the world, the windward capabilities of the boat are not crucial, but if one intends to do a lot of zigzagging across the weather systems, a boat that can go well to windward is essential. A powerful and reliable engine can be just as important if one intends to explore out of the way places and reef areas. A moderate draft can also prove to be an advantage in such areas, as could the choice of a multihull.

After writing about the loss of cruising boats, I have been often asked about the safety of small boat voyaging. It is of course impossible to assess the overall safety of small boat voyaging, but the onus of safe cruising lies very much in the hands of each individual. Exactly as in motoring, where one can minimise the chances of an accident by driving carefully, taking avoiding action in good time, obeying the rules of the road and having a safe car, so on a boat one can apply the same principles, with the added advantage that most of the time one's life is not put at risk by the bad driving habits of others. After thousands of miles and many years of sailing, I have reached the conclusion that sailing is as safe as we ourselves make it, because ultimately the safety of our lives is most of the time in our own hands. In the words of the Welsh poet, W. H. Davies,

> 'I am the Master of my fate.
> I am the Captain of my soul.'

Being the master of one's own fate is for me one of the main attractions of long distance cruising.

The Surveys

1. THE SUVA SURVEY

No.	Name of Boat	Home Port	Country	Design	Rig	Mat	LOD	Crew	Place most liked
1	Eryx II	Gibraltar	Gibraltar	Camper & Nich.	Sc	S	78	4	Marquesas
2	Constellation	San Diego	USA	Alden	Sc	W	76	8	Fiji
3	Mandalay	Seattle	USA	R. Perry CT 54	K/s	G	54	3	Philippines
4	Spellbound II	Dartmouth	UK	A. Buchanen	K/s	W	52	3	Galapagos
5	Merry Maiden	Boston	USA	P. Rhodes	K	W	52	4	Easter Island
6	La Bohême	San Francisco	USA	Force 50	K/s	G	51	4	Lesser Antilles
7	Integrity	Hawaii	USA	E. McInnes	K	W	50	5	Tahiti
8	Mac's Opal	Coos Bay	USA	Samson Seabreeze	K/s	F	49'9	2	Ahe
9	Mortail	San Francisco	USA	Guy Beach/tri	K	P	47	3	Fiji
10	Enchantress	Hawaii	USA	Wellington 47	K/s	G	47	5	Fiji
11	Galatea IV	Vancouver	Canada	C. Kennedy	C	G	47	3	Vava'u
12	Sea Swan	New York	USA	A. Corener	Sc	W	46'6	3	Tahiti
13	Antigone	San Francisco	USA	Piver 46/tri	K	P	46	4	Vava'u
14	Con Tina	Los Angeles	USA	Cal 2-46	K	G	46	2	Bora Bora
15	Jolly II Roger	Portland	USA	Cal 2-46	K	G	46	2	W. Samoa
16	Whistler	Lyons	USA	Cal 2-46	K	G	46	2	Suvorov
17	Honeymead	Brisbane	Australia	Roberts Offshore	K/s	G	44	2	Alaska
18	Norseman	Long Beach	USA	Block Island	C	W	42	2	Hawaii
19	Aminadab	Santa Barbara	USA	Westsail	C	G	42	2	Tahiti
20	Rhodora	Key West	USA	R. Perry	C	G	42	2	Papua New Guinea
21	Caravela of Exe	Exeter	UK	Alden 42	Y	G	42	2	Fiji
22	Sarrie	Auckland	NZ	CT 41	K	G	41	4	Spain
23	Kaunis Uni	Juno	USA	Piver AA/tri	Sl	P	41	3	Alaska

No.	Name of Boat	Home Port	Country	Design	Rig	Mat	LOD	Crew	Place most liked
24	Hägar	Sydney	Australia	J. Adams	C	S	40	2	Suvorov
25	Fair Lady	San Francisco	USA	L. Giles	C	W	40	3	Fiji
26	Tikitere	Auckland	NZ	B. Donovan	K/s	F	40	2	Fiji
27	Whale's Tale II	Hawaii	USA	Islander 40	K	G	40	4	Fiji
28	Gitana del Mar	San Diego	USA	Garden Gulf	Sl	G	40	3	Rarotonga
29	Camdella	Napier	NZ	Herreshoff	Sl	W	38	3	Makongai/Fiji
30	Riptide	Kimbe	PNG	S & S 38	Sl	A	38	3	Carolines
31	Akahi	Hawaii	USA	Cross 38/tri	K	W	38	2	Costa Rica
32	Taurewa	Nelson	NZ	R. Perry	C	G	37	2	Fiji
33	Hero	Portsmouth	USA	Mariner 36	C	G	36	2	Hawaii
34	Spindrift	Melbourne	Australia	Almsemgeeste	C	S	36	4	Fiji
35	Active Light	Pt. Townsend	USA	Atkin Tallyho	C	G	36	2	Vava'u
36	Coryphena	San Diego	USA	Hanna Carol	K	W	36	2	Suvorov
37	Sea Foam	Newport Beach	USA	Seawitch	K/s	W	36	3	Suvorov
38	Sea Rover	Manele/Hawaii	USA	Seawitch	K/s	W	36	2	Papeete
39	Super Roo II	Newport Beach	USA	Eriksson 36	C	G	36	4	Lord Howe
40	Swan	Portland	USA	Cascade 36	Sl	G	36	2	Vava'u
41	Warna Carina	Perth	Australia	Randall	K	F	36	5	Indonesia
42	Karak	Morlaix	France	Knocker	K	S	35'6	2	Lesser Antilles
43	Windrose	Vancouver	Canada	Nicholson 35	Sl	G	35'3	2	San Blas
44	Banjeeri	Newcastle	Australia	Randall	Sl	S	35	2	New Zealand
45	Lorbas	Köln	Germany	Kirk	Sl	G	35	2	Tuamotus
46	Olive Marie	Oxnard	USA	Garden 35	K/s	G	35	2	New Hebrides
47	Ranger	Victoria	Canada	Garden 35	K/s	W	35	2	French Polynesia
48	UFO II	Arnhem	Netherlands	Telstar/tri	Sl	G	35	2	Madeira
49	No name	Hawaii	USA	Robb 35	Sl	G	35	3	Suvorov
50	Hibiscus	Witianga	NZ	Woolacott	K/s	W	34	2	North Island/NZ

No.	Name	Port	Country	Designer	Rig	Material	Length	Crew	Destination
51	Jocelyn	Newport Beach	USA	Lapworth	Sl	G	33'3	2	Tahiti
52	Kemana	Vancouver	Canada	Brewer 32	Sl	G	32	2	Ahe
53	Noa Noa	Miami	USA	P. Rhodes	K	W	32	2	Suvorov
54	Horizon	Stowe	USA	Golden Hind	Sl	P	31'6	3	Marquesas
55	Lou IV	Elmshorn	Germany	Jensen	K	G	31	2	Moorea
56	Runestaff	Whangerei	NZ	Herreshoff	C	G	29'7	2	Aitutaki
57	Ben Gunn	Wellington	NZ	Herreshoff	Sl	G	29	2	Virginia
58	Pink Mola Mola	Tokyo	Japan	Nakayoshi	Sl	G	28'9	1	Bora Bora
59	Alonda	Brisbane	Australia	Hartley Tasman	Sl	F	27'3	2	Fiji
60	Sara III	Stockholm	Sweden	Grinde	Sl	G	27	2	Galapagos
61	Lookfar	Seattle	USA	Westerly Centaur	Sl	G	26	2	Lau/Fiji
62	Jonathan	San Francisco	USA	Columbia	Sl	G	24	2	Palmyra

Rig: K = ketch
K/s = staysail ketch
Sc = schooner
Sl = sloop
C = cutter
Y = yawl

Material: S = steel
G = fibreglass or foam sandwich
W = wood
P = plywood
F = ferrocement
A = light alloy

2. THE CRUISING SURVEY

No.	Name of boat	Home Port	Country	Design	Rig	LOD	Crew	Length of cruise Yrs	Miles	Skipper
1	Orplid	Bremen	Germany	One off	K	56	2	3	22000	Rolf Stukenberg
2	Starshine	San Francisco	USA	Own	K	56	2+1	1½	8000	Doug Balcombe
3	Wanderlust	Sacramento	USA	Veleo 55	C	55	6	1½	10000	Steve Carter
4	Merry Maiden	Boston	USA	P. Rhodes	K	52	4	10	50000	Seaton Grass
5	Wanderer IV	Southampton	UK	Van der Meer	K	50	2	11	70000	Eric Hiscock
6	Mac's Opal	Coos Bay	USA	Seabreeze	K	50	2	3	30000	Royal McInness
7	Diogenes	Portland	USA	O. Stephens	K	50	3	5	48000	Gustaf Wollmar
8	Duen	St. Thomas/VI	USA	Norwegian FV	K	48	2+2	8	50000	Albert Fletcher
9	Hawk	Miami	USA	Adams	Sc	48	2	1½	18000	Dud Dewey
10	Alkinoos	La Rochelle	France	Nicholson 48	K	48	2	3	24000	Jean-Fr. Delvaux
11	Galatea IV	Vancouver	Canada	C. Kennedy	C	47	3	1½	10000	Bob Miller
12	Roscop	Antwerp	Belgium	Martens	K	46	2	2½	15000	Rein Mortier
13	Korong II	Brisbane	Australia	Own	K	43	2+2	2	10000	John Holmes
14	Canard Laqué	Basle	Switzerland	Luders Clipper	K	42	2	8	55000	Pierre Graf
15	Aslan	San Diego	USA	Kettenburg	Sl	41	2	2	10000	Scott Wilmoth
16	Shangri-La	Hamburg	Germany	Hartz/cat	K	40	3	2	23000	Burghard Pieske
17	Hägar	Sydney	Australia	J. Adams	C	40	2	4	20000	Gunter Gross
18	Calao	Toulon	France	Finisterre	Y	40	2+2	3	22000	Erick Bouteleux
19	Wrangler	Durban	South Africa	Own	K	40	2	2	22000	Robert Millar
20	Tarrawarra	Melbourne	Australia	A. Payne	Sl	38	3	2	12000	Kim Prowd
21	Felix	Paimpol	France	Ophelie	K	38	2+1	3	25000	Alain Bloch

22	Incognito	Santa Barbara	USA	One off	Sl	38	2	5	22000	Steve Abney
23	Rising Sun	Los Angeles	USA	Lapworth	Sl	37	2	2	10000	Dan Bache-Wiig
24	Fortuna	Auckland	NZ	One off	C	37	2+2	7	50000	Mike Morrish
25	Peregrine	San Diego	USA	Berthan Gauntlet	C	37	1	$3\frac{1}{2}$	12000	Albert Steele
26	Gambol	Tauranga	NZ	One off	Sl	37	2	6	45000	Stuart Clay
27	Hero	Portsmouth	USA	R. Perry	C	36	2	2	10000	Richard Holcombe
28	Because	Victoria	Canada	One off	C	36	1	$1\frac{1}{2}$	10000	Dick Thulliers
29	Tern	Knysna	South Africa	One off	Sl	36	1	2	23000	John Travers
30	Sea Foam	Newport Beach	USA	Seawitch	K	36	3	$6\frac{1}{2}$	35000	Herb Payson
31	Karak	Morlaix	France	Knocker	K	35	2	$3\frac{1}{2}$	21000	Georges Calmé
32	Windrose	Vancouver	Canada	Nicholson 35	Sl	35	2	2	20000	Mik Madsen
33	Ranger	Victoria	Canada	Garden	K	35	2	3	14000	Gene Williams
34	Telemark	Southampton	UK	Buchanan Yeoman	Sl	35	2	12	50000	Alan Allmark
35	Jocelyn	Newport Beach	USA	Cal 34	Sl	33	2	2	10000	Jay Becker
36	Iemanja	San Francisco	USA	Luders	K	33	2	$1\frac{1}{2}$	15000	Grant Nielson
37	Potpourri	Hueneme	USA	Islander	C	32	2	1	10000	Al Huso
38	L'Orion	San Francisco	USA	Westsail	C	32	2+1	$1\frac{1}{2}$	8000	Don Lewis
39	Talofa Lee	San Francisco	USA	Westsail	C	32	2	1	10000	Dave Weikart
40	Kemana	Vancouver	Canada	Brewer	Sl	32	2	3	14000	Nick Zeldenrust
41	Spaciety	San Diego	USA	Kantola/tri	Sl	32	2	6	30000	Larry Pooter
42	Horizon	Stowe	USA	Golden Hind	Sl	31	2+1	$1\frac{1}{2}$	15000	Bruce MacDonald
43	Lou IV	Elmshorn	Germany	Jensen	K	31	2	3	30000	Herbert Gieseking
44	Tehani III	Antwerp	Belgium	West Hinder	Sl	31	1	2	23000	Jan Swerts
45	Macushlah	Honolulu	USA	Kittiwake	K	30	2	9	12000	Dave Malseed

No.	Name of boat	Home Port	Country	Design	Rig	LOD	Crew	Length of cruise Yrs	Miles	Skipper
46	Fawn of Chichester	Cowes	UK	Cavalier	Sl	30	2	2	20000	Roger Morgan
47	Runestaff	Whangerei	NZ	Herreshoff	C	29	2	4	16000	Ian Hancock
48	Tara II	Vancouver	Canada	Vancouver	Sl	27	2	2	8000	George Hartley
49	Silverheels	San Diego	USA	Yankee	Sl	26	2	1½	8000	David Mancini
50	Jellicle	South Shields	UK	Folkboat	C	25	2	20	85000	Mike Bailes

Rig:
K = ketch
C = cutter
Sc = schooner
Sl = sloop
Y = yawl

3. THE SEAWIVES SURVEY

No.	Name	Country	Boat	LOD	Yrs Present Cruise	Children on board Names (age)
1	Ruth Abney	NZ	Incognito	38	5	
2	Beryl Allmark	UK	Telemark	35	12	
3	Denny Bache-Wiig	USA	Rising Sun	37	2	
4	Linda Balcombe	USA	Starshine	56	$1\frac{1}{2}$	Heather (11)
5	Kathy Becker	USA	Jocelyn	33	2	
6	Betty Bloch	France	Felix	38	3	Yann (5)
7	Muriel Bouteleux	France	Calao	40	3	Sidonie (8), Fabien (5)
8	Hélène Calmé	France	Karak	35	$3\frac{1}{2}$	
9	Pamela Church	Zimbabwe	Gambol	37	3	
10	Jeannette Delvaux	France	Alkinoos	48	3	
11	Barbara Dewey	USA	Hawk	48	$1\frac{1}{2}$	
12	Dottie Fletcher	USA	Duen	48	8	Toby (13), James (11)
13	Illa Gieseking	Germany	Lou IV	31	3	
14	Ute Graf	Switzerland	Canard Laqué	42	8	
15	Derry Hancock	UK	Runestaff	29	4	Tristan (6 weeks)
16	Cynthia Hathaway	USA	Spaciety	32	2	
17	Suzanne Hartley	Canada	Tara II	27	2	
18	Susan Hiscock	UK	Wanderer IV	50	11	
19	Vicki Holmes	Australia	Korong II	43	2	Kirsty (5), Denby (3)
20	Karen Huso	USA	Potpourri	32	1	
21	Nancy Lewis	USA	L'Orion	32	$1\frac{1}{2}$	Daren (8)
22	Kay Malseed	USA	Macushlah	30	9	

No.	Name	Country	Boat	LOD	Yrs present Cruise	Children on board Names (age)
23	Pat Mancini	USA	Silverheels	26	$1\frac{1}{2}$	
24	Lorraine Millar	South Africa	Wrangler	40	2	
25	Marg Miller	Canada	Galatea IV	47	1	
26	Anne Morrish	NZ	Fortuna	37	7	Paul (13), Tina (11)
27	Marie-Louise Mortier	Belgium	Roscop	46	$2\frac{1}{2}$	
28	Liz MacDonald	USA	Horizon	31	$1\frac{1}{2}$	Jeff (10)
29	D'Ann McLain	USA	Windrose	35	2	
30	Opal McInness	USA	Mac's Opal	50	3	
31	Donna Nielson	USA	Iemanja	32	1	
32	Nancy Payson	USA	Sea Foam	36	$6\frac{1}{2}$	
33	Carol Ritz	USA	Hero	36	2	
34	Helga Seebeck	Germany	Shangri-La	40	2	
35	Alice Simpson	UK	Fawn of Chichester	30	2	
36	Stefani Stukenberg	Germany	Orplid	56	3	
37	Blitz Weikart	USA	Talofa Lee	32	1	
38	Marie Williams	Canada	Ranger	35	3	
39	Beverly Wilmoth	USA	Aslan	41	2	
40	Britz Zeldenrust	Canada	Kemana	32	3	

4. THE PACIFIC SEAWIVES SURVEY

No.	Name	Country	Boat	LOD	Yrs present Cruise	Children on board Names (age)
1	Sylvia Beaurivage	Canada	Drummer	32	2	
2	Pierrette Benoidt	Belgium	Ondine	36	5	
3	Marge Bryson	USA	Ave del Mar	30	2	Stuart (12)
4	Nina Cadle	USA	Abuelo III	35	5	Luisa (3), Juanito (1)
5	Betty Eastman	USA	Con Tina	46	8	
6	Liisa Einarsson	Sweden	Irma	30	4	
7	Alice Fabre	France	Drac II	51	12	
8	Anne Faubert	France	Kouros	42	2	Peggy (11), Franklin (4)
9	Madeleine Fily	France	Stereden Vor	47	4	Emmanuelle (16)
10	Madeleine Gagnant	France	Apoutziak	32	3	
11	Susanna Graveleau	Argentina	Hispania	50	3	Carlos (4)
12	Marika Hantel	Germany	Pytheas	40	6	Eric (7), Benedict (3)
13	Anne Hutton	New Zealand	Chanceegger	63	1	
14	Jutta Jung	Germany	Jeux à Deux	34	4	
15	Anna Kass	Germany	Bellatrix	38	14	
16	Irmtraud Klein	Germany	Haubaut	40	4	
17	Bärbel Kurz	Germany	Atair II	43	4	
18	Betty Lowe	Great Britain	Windrace	36	1	
19	June Macauley	USA	Acheta	38	3	
20	Chantal Martin	France	El Djezair	37	2	Corinne (16)
21	Nancy McKeown	USA	Shanachie	46	2	
22	Marg Mitchell	USA	Whale Song	40	3	
23	Velda Moore	USA	Prospector	43	3	
24	Dana Nicholson	Antigua	Spray	34	2	
25	Linda Pearse	Tahiti	Vahine Rii	36	1	Jimmy (6), Mareva (4)

No. Name	Country	Boat	LOD	Yrs present Cruise	Children on board Names (age)
26 Nancy Pihl	USA	Moon River	35	8	
27 Cristina Plantier	Italy	Madame Bertrand	33	3	
28 Janice Pickering	Canada	Northern Chinook	38	2	
29 Margaret Pickering	Great Britain	Keegenoo	32	5	
30 Dorine Samuelson	France	Swan II	43	5	Nicky (6)
31 Hana Sauzier	Mauritius	Vanessa	37	13	
32 Sheri Schneider	USA	Moli	33	4	
33 Pascale Simon	France	Kalabush	40	4	Colin (6 mths)
34 Sri Sukaesih	Indonesia	Dumeklemmer II	40	2	Marcus (6), Matari (5)
35 Monique Tournier	France	Volte	38	5	Yannik (8), Ronan (6)
36 Marianne Trisdale	USA	Pelargic II	31	3	
37 Elizabeth Veuve	Switzerland	Penelope	32	5	
38 Saskia Whitehead	Holland	Cornelia	46	5	
39 Marion Zech	Switzerland	Spirit of Cockpit	48	4	
40 Maria van Zelderen	Holland	White Pointer	41	10	Ronald (16), Edith (14)

5. THE CIRCUMNAVIGATORS SURVEY

No.	Boat	Crew	Country	Design	LOA	Material	Rig	Years	Mileage	Favourite Place
1	Alkinoos	Jeannette & Jean-François Delvaux	France	Camper & Nicholson	48	GRP	K	4½	45,000	Lesser Antilles
2	Barsoi	Heinz Lutz	Germany	S & S	30	GRP	Sl	4	36,000	French Polynesia
3	Ben Gunn	Tony Ray Kevin Oliver	NZ	Herreshoff	28	GRP	Sl	4	40,000	Virginia, USA
4	Gambol	Stuart Clay (Pam Church)	NZ	T. Coyte	37	W	Sl	6	40,000	Virgin Islands
5	Horizon	Liz & Bruce MacDonald & son Jeff	USA	Golden Hind	31	GRP on ply	Sl	3	33,500	Indonesia
6	Kyeri	Herb & Mary-Louise Stewart	USA	Hinckley-Owens	40	W	C	3	35,000	New Zealand
7	Lorbas	Achim & Irma Geysel	Germany	Amel	36	GRP	Sl	3	29,000	Tuamotus
8	Lou IV	Herbert & Ilse Gieseking	Germany	Compass Jensen	31	GRP	K	4½	46,000	Solomon Islands
9	Pomona	Ian & Sylvia French & son John	UK	Colin Cowen	27	W	Sl	3	31,000	Cocos Keeling
10	Sara III	Christer & Britt Fredriksson	Sweden	P. Bruun	26	GRP	Sl	5	50,000	Melanesia
11	Tivia	Doncho & Julie Papazov & daughter Yana	Bulgaria	Polish one off	45	W	K	2	40,500	French Polynesia
12	Windrose	Mik Madsen (D'Ann McLain)	Canada	Nicholson	35	GRP	Sl	3¼	47,000	San Blas

6. THE PACIFIC SURVEY 1984

No.	Name of boat	Design/Designer	LOD (ft)	(m)	Rig	Material	Country	Mileage on present cruise	Where interviewed
1	Chanceegger	International 12m	63	19	Sl	W	France (NZ crew)	16,000	Opua
2	Drac II	Auzepi-Brenner	51	15.5	K/s	W	France	100,000	Raiatea
3	Hispania	Mauric	50	15	K/s	W	France	20,000	Whangarei
4	Spirit of Cockpit	Cheoy Lee 48	48	14	K/s	F	Hong Kong (Swiss crew)	22,000	Papeete
5	Stereden Vor	Lex Eterna	47	14	Sc	S	France	17,000	Opua
6	Con Tina	Cal 2–46	46	13.8	K	F	USA	20,000	Noumea
7	Shanachie	Whiting 46	46	13.8	Sl	W	USA	14,000	Opua
8	Cornelia	Buchanan	46	13.8	K	S	Holland	26,000	Opua
9	Prospector	Concordia	43	13	Y	W	USA	16,000	Opua
10	Swan II	Swan 43	43	13	Sl	F	Hawaii (GB/Fr crew)	20,000	Papeete
11	Atair II	Colin Archer	43	13	K/s	S	Germany	17,000	Opua
12	Kouros	Jade 42	42	12.6	Sl	Al	France	23,000	Opua
13	Spanish Eyes	Formosa 42	42	12.6	K/s	F	Hong Kong (Australian crew)	47,000	Opua
14	White Pointer	Bluejacket	41	12.3	K/s	S	Australia (Dutch crew)	90,000	Raiatea
15	Jenelle	Westsail 43	41	12.3	K/s	F	USA	10,000	Opua
16	Dolcelle	Salar 40	40	12	Sl	W	Great Britain	18,000	Papeete
17	Dumeklemmer II	Rasbora 120	40	12	K	S	Germany	18,000	Papeete
18	Barfly	Sun fizz 40	40	12	Sl	F	Great Britain (Australian crew)	10,000	Papeete
19	Kalabush	Friedjen	40	12	Sl	S	France	17,000	Papeete
20	Haubaut	Maxi 120	40	12	K	F	Germany	26,000	Opua
21	Whale Song	Edwin Monk	40	12	C	W	USA	15,000	Opua
22	Pytheas	Dutch Pilot Cutter	40	12	C	S	Germany	28,000	Opua
23	Volte	Rêve D'Antilles	38	11.5	Sl	S	France	14,000	Raiatea
24	Bellatrix	Illingworth	38	11.5	Sl	W	Sweden	45,000	Opua
25	Northern Chinook	Roberts 38	38	11.5	C	F	Canada	10,000	Opua

#	Name	LOA	Rig	Material	Country	Price	Port
26	Acheta	38	C	F	USA	13,000	Opua
27	Vanessa	37	Sl	W	Mauritius	35,000	Raiatea
28	Spe-Ow	37	C	F	France	25,000	Papeete
29	El Djezair	37	K	F	France	12,000	Papeete
30	Ondine	36	Sl	F	Belgium	30,000	Opua
31	Vahine Rii	36	C	S	Australia	7,000	Whangarei
32	Windrace	36	Sl	F	Great Britain	14,000	Auckland
33	Moon River	35	Y	W	USA	30,000	Opua
34	Abuelo III	35	K/s	F	Spain	25,000	Opua
35	Nightwing	35	C	S	Canada	10,000	Opua
36	Spray	34	Sl	W	USA	12,000	Opua
37	Jeux à Deux	34	Sl	S	Germany	35,000	Opua
38	Moli	33	C	W	USA	14,000	Opua
39	Grendel	33	C	S	USA	9,000	Whangarei
40	Madame Bertrand Aquavit	33	Sl	W	France	25,000	Raiatea
41	Palma	32	C	F	Denmark	30,000	Papeete
42	Christopher Robin Westsail 32	32	C	F	USA	14,000	Opua
43	Drummer	32	C	F	Canada	10,000	Opua
44	Penelope	32	K/s	S	Switzerland	25,000	Raiatea
45	Keegenoo	32	Sl	F	Great Britain	25,000	Auckland
46	Apoutziak	31.5	Sl	S	France	12,000	Papeete
47	Pelargic II	31	C	F	USA	13,000	Opua
48	Irma	30	K/s	W	Sweden	24,000	Whangarei
49	Ave del Mar	30	Sl	F	USA	16,000	Opua
50	Jellicle	25	Sl	W	Great Britain	100,000	Opua

Additional name column (boat designs):

#	Design
26	Hans Christian
27	Vanessa
28	Tristmus
29	Gib Sea 37
30	Bowman 36
31	Buchanan
32	Rustler 36
33	Coastwise cruiser
34	Endurance 35
35	John Hutton
36	Peter Norlin
37	Roberts 34
38	Colin Archer
39	John Boaz
40	Francois Graeser
41	Westsail 32
42	Westsail 32
43	Westsail 32
44	Francois Graeser
45	Yachting World Barbican
46	Keragan
47	Cape George 31
48	Tahiti ketch
49	Rawson 30
50	Folkboat

Rig: C = Cutter
K = Ketch
K/s = Staysail ketch
Sc = Schooner
Sl = Sloop
Y = Yawl

Material: Al = Aluminium
F = Fibreglass
S = Steel
W = Wood

Index